"THE RULES is not ju~~~~~~~~~~~~~~
—~~~~~

And now praise for the

# THE RULES™ II

"The Rules are just for dating, right? Wrong. In their new book, THE RULES II, Ellen Fein and Sherrie Schneider address the questions their readers have posed—including . . . tips on how to make any marriage better, happier, stronger."
—*Bridal Guide*

"We're not talking about a business deal here, but getting the man you want to propose and then to turn that proposal into an actual wedding date— it's a feat some women would say can be tougher than any corporate transaction. Of course, it's made much easier by doing The Rules."
—*Complete Woman*

"Empowering. . . . The Rules books can give you control over your dating life."
—*Mademoiselle*

"Drumroll, please, for single-and-searching females! More help is here in THE RULES II, the sequel to THE RULES, the runaway *New York Times* bestseller."
—*San Antonio Express-News*

*more . . .*

# RICE AND BOUQUETS FOR THE #1 BESTSELLER
## THE RULES

"There is a certain kind of woman who is given to long tousled hair, sheer black panty hose, and acting maddeningly elusive to every man. . . . She is breezy, confident, and independent, as well as coy, manipulative, and very, very hard to get. She is a Rules Girl."

*—New York Times*

"A must-read for . . . women seeking success in romance."

*—People*

"If you're a single woman trying to keep your own life from becoming a soap opera, then THE RULES has something to tell you."

*—New Jersey Monthly*

"A lot of good advice. . . . Friends should read the book together, discuss The Rules and the reasons for them and encourage each other to stick to The Rules. They may laugh at first, but if they follow The Rules, it will take a lot of stress off themselves, allow them to be happier in their lives, and pave the way for a lasting relationship with a man who does the pursuing—and feels rewarded when he catches the woman he adores."

—*Baton Rouge Sunday Advocate*

"Waiting around is certainly not what Ellen Fein and Sherrie Schneider have in mind. Their message is clear: It's to the battlefields. Arm yourself and become a full-time Rules Girl! Practice them! Memorize the book! Make him pursue you until you catch him! And live life happily ever after. Amen."

—*Detroit News*

"Lighthearted yet earnest. . . . Even if you're engaged or married, you still need these guidelines."

—*Jerusalem Post Literary Supplement*

# ALSO BY THE AUTHORS

THE RULES

THE RULES DATING JOURNAL

THE RULES NOTE CARDS

Published by
WARNER BOOKS

# THE RULES II

## More Rules to Live and Love By

ELLEN FEIN
AND SHERRIE SCHNEIDER

**WARNER BOOKS**

A Time Warner Company

Author Note:

"We are not licensed to practice psychology, psychiatry, or social work, and *The Rules* is not intended to replace psychological counseling, but is simply a dating philosophy based on our own experiences and those of thousands of women who have contacted us."

Portions of Chapter 27 first appeared in *Ladies' Home Journal*.

WARNER BOOKS EDITION

*Cover design by Diane Luger*
*Cover illustration by Nancy Palubniak*
*Book design by Giorgetta Bell McRee*

Warner Books, Inc.
1271 Avenue of the Americas
New York, NY 10020

Visit our Web site at
www.warnerbooks.com

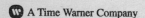 A Time Warner Company

Printed in the United States of America
Originally published in hardcover by Warner Books.
First printed in paperback: September, 1998

10 9 8

# Acknowledgments

We would like to thank our wonderful husbands and children for their love and support.

Special thanks, too, to our agent Stedman Mays at Connie Clausen & Associates.

A big thank you to everyone at Warner Books, in particular Chairman of Time Warner Trade Publishing Larry Kirshbaum, our Editor Caryn Karmatz Rudy, Senior Publicist Tina Andreadis, and Publicity Assistant Heather Fain.

And, of course, we owe our thanks to our mothers Sylvia and Margie, our friends, our staff, Rules contacts around the world, and the thousands of women who wrote and called and encouraged us to wrote *The Rules II*. Most of all, we dedicate this book to the memory of Connie Clausen, our literary agent and friend.

Ellen and Sherrie

# Contents

# THE
# RULES II

# Foreword: *The Rules* Phenomenon

Four years ago, when we set out to write *The Rules,* we knew that we had an important message to share. We believed in *The Rules.* We had seen them work time and time again in our own lives, in our close circle of girlfriends and an ever-widening circle of friends and acquaintances, as well as coworkers and relatives.

When our phones began ringing off the hook with dating questions and (eventually) success stories, we knew we had to write *The Rules* in book form to make it available to *all* women.

Lo and behold, *The Rules* became not just a best-selling book, but a phenomenon, revolutionizing dating practices both here in America and abroad.

In fact, *The Rules* became so popular that it achieved a kind of pop culture status. It was spoofed on *Saturday Night Live* ("Get the ring!"), used as the plot for several TV sitcoms, and also inspired a number of parody books

1

including *Breaking the Rules* ("Stare straight at men and talk incessantly") and *Rules for Cats* ("Don't accept a trip to the vet after Wednesday").

Suddenly, *The Rules* was everywhere! A financial publication ran an article on the rules for investing ("Don't buy on Friday if your broker calls after Wednesday") and a political columnist wrote that one presidential candidate might have won the election if he had just tried to be a "creature unlike any other."

Why all the fuss? Why all the interest in *The Rules* when there are dozens of other dating books on the market? Why has *The Rules* become such a phenomenon?

The answer is simple: *The Rules* work! Unlike other dating books that are therapeutic and theoretical—that sound good, that give warm 'n fuzzy, meaningless, and misleading advice such as *be yourself, don't play games, tell a man how you feel,* but don't work in real life—*The Rules* tell the truth about dating and help you get Mr. Right!

*The Rules* take the analysis and angst out of dating. It's simple. If he calls you, he likes you. If he doesn't, *Next!* What does *be yourself* mean if that's calling a man three times a day or staying on the phone for three hours? Why would anyone want to read a dating book that didn't help you get the man you want to marry you?

Many people ask how we wrote a best-seller. To be honest, we were not trying to. We wrote *The Rules* to help women date with self-esteem and get married. Period.

While we are naturally thrilled by the success of the book, what's been even more rewarding is seeing how women of all ages and all walks of life use *The Rules* to love themselves and marry Mr. Right. After three decades of haphazard dating—dutch treat, sex on the first date, and living together—these women are delighted that such a dating book exists.

"I wish I had known about *The Rules* ten years ago," is the most frequent comment we hear.

"*The Rules* should be given out to all women at birth," wrote another *Rules* fan.

The book hit a chord not only with single women in their twenties, thirties, and forties, but with mothers and grandmothers. "She won't listen to me, maybe she'll listen to you," wrote one mom. Another mom told us she gave the book to her daughter and her daughter's friends.

While many readers thanked us for the general guidelines provided in *The Rules,* just as many wrote and called asking for more specific answers to dating situations and problems—for example, rules for long-distance relationships, rules for getting back an ex-boyfriend, rules for dating a celebrity, rules for dating a coworker, rules for turning a male friend into a boyfriend, rules for dating services and on-line dating, and for advice on how to start a *Rules* support group, among many other topics.

We wrote *The Rules II* to answer all these questions—and to clarify any confusion you might have about rules in the first book, such as, "How will he know the real me if I do *The Rules*?" and "Can I *ever* call a man?"

We have included some success stories in *The Rules II*

that we hope will inspire you to do *The Rules.* We hope to publish many more—perhaps yours!—in the future.

We look forward to your comments, questions, success stories, and wedding invitations!

Ellen and Sherrie

*Chapter 1* _____

# Why *The Rules* Work

Why do *The Rules* work?

Because *The Rules* are based upon the basic truths of human nature! Everyone wishes we could be more open and honest with men in the early stages of dating or ask men out, but these wishes are pure fantasy. To think men and women should treat each other exactly alike, as platonic friends do—dutch treat, even steven, tit for tat—is unrealistic. In the *romantic* world, there's only one way that truly works. The man must be attracted to and then pursue the woman. It simply doesn't work any other way.

That doesn't mean we have to *like* it. Even *we* didn't want *The Rules* to be true. Who wants it to be true that a man's attraction to us doesn't grow? Who wants it to be true that a man might lose interest if we're too aggressive, too needy, or too predictable?

Everyone wishes certain things were different from what they are. Who wants war, crime, or bitter cold weather?

5

Who wants to diet and exercise? Wouldn't it be great if we could eat whatever we wanted, whenever we felt like it and still be slim, fit, and have perfect thighs?

*Rules* girls are realists. They accept that men and women are different and act accordingly. They don't always *like* to do The Rules, but they do them anyway because they love the results.

Of course, as popular as *The Rules* has become, it has also been the subject of controversy—mostly by the media and the authors of other dating books, not by women who simply want advice about men. They just want to get married!

*The Rules* have been criticized for being old-fashioned and antifeminist, and for encouraging women to play games and get married at any cost ("get the ring"). We would like to examine these criticisms one by one and explain why they are unfounded.

Old-fashioned? Not really. While *The Rules* may sound like something your mother may have told you about, times and circumstances have completely changed. Women in the '90s need *The Rules*—not because pursuing men is morally wrong or scandalous, or any of the reasons your mother may have told you. No, *The Rules* tell us not to pursue men for one simple reason. It doesn't work!

Fifty years ago, women didn't call men or live with men before marriage because it was considered socially unacceptable. Fifty years ago, they didn't even need to think about "ending the date first." Their fathers ended it for them by requiring them to be home at a certain time, much like their great-grandfathers put an end to dates by holding up a shotgun on the front porch!

In addition, back then, women often had to get married in order to move out of their parents' house. Women were financially dependent on men, and once married they became full-time wives and mothers who, for the most part, did not pursue careers.

Compare that to '90s women. Many are financially self-sufficient. They can afford their own apartments, cars, vacations, wardrobes, and creature comforts. They can even have or adopt and support a child on their own. They no longer need men to get away from their parents or to have good or interesting lives. But the truth is they *want* men in their lives—as partners/friends, lovers, husbands/fathers. They can function without men, but they yearn for marriage and children and/or fulfilling relationships.

Their problem is *how* to get married or be in fulfilling relationships. The sexual revolution of the '60s proved to be filled with empty promises—sex and living together did not add up to commitment.

Who or what can women turn to for dating advice? They may or may not be able to relate to their mothers. Besides, some mothers, trying to be hip and modern or desperate for their daughters to get married and produce a grandchild, will give them bad advice and tell them to call men and pay their own way. ("Don't be so picky," they tell them.)

Their female friends, conditioned by the social mores of today and with well-meaning intentions, may say "Oh, call him if you like him! What have you got to lose?" If he turns them down, "So, what?" they say.

Well, we say:

(1) Maybe if you don't call him, he'll build up a *real* desire and call you!

(2) A man who is receptive to your advances (without making any of his own) may date or even marry you at your suggestion, but down the road he'll be bored and ambivalent toward you.

Women have turned to *The Rules* because it's the only advice they can count on that works. They're not retro, they're fabulous!

Antifeminist? No, as far as we are concerned, there is no conflict between *The Rules* and feminism. *Rules* girls can be feminists. *We are feminists.* We believe in and are grateful for the advances women have made in the last century. How else could we have become authors and formed a company? All women have different definitions of feminism, but to us, it is about getting equal pay for equal work. It's about women being authors, astronauts, doctors, lawyers, CEOs, or whatever they want to be— getting promoted, being treated the same and paid as much as men!

Feminism is also about women believing in their own importance. It is about being fulfilled by our jobs, our hobbies, our friendships. It is knowing that the women in our lives are as important as the men—and treating our friends with respect and consideration to prove it!

But with all due respect, feminism has not changed men or the nature of romantic relationships. Like it or not, men are emotionally and romantically different from women. Men are biologically the aggressor. They thrive on challenge—whether it's the stock market, basketball, or football—while women crave security and bonding. This has been true since civilization began!

Men who respond to *The Rules* are not sick or stupid, but quite normal and healthy. Your average guy. What would be *sick* is if a man chased and chased a woman who clearly didn't want him, who repeatedly said "no" when he asked her out as early as Monday for Saturday night. But that's not what we're talking about. We're talking about a woman who says "yes" to dates when asked a few days in advance and is nice to men on dates. She's simply not too eager and doesn't drop everything to see him at a moment's notice. That way he respects her and wants to be with her and marry her.

*Why* men are naturally driven by challenge is not important. The point is to do what works to have a successful relationship, which is to let men do the pursuing . . . in other words, to follow *The Rules*.

After twenty to thirty years of do-what-you-feel and haphazard dating, most women we know are actually relieved to have rules and boundaries to live by. These women are happy that feminism has helped them get ahead in business and given them financial independence, but they agree that trying to be as aggressive in relationships with men as they are in their careers doesn't work.

Are we telling women to play games? Some people like to focus on the most superficial aspects in *The Rules*—the ones most likely to promote controversy—but the book is really about self-esteem, about setting boundaries. Yes, in some ways, you're playing a game. The game is called *liking yourself*! The game is not accepting just any treatment from a man. The game is being true to your heart. Everyone knows in their hearts that *The Rules* work, that this is the way it really is. But some people have to read the book a few times before they get the message that it's not just about egg timers, lipstick, and not returning calls.

*The Rules* is not an etiquette book—it's not about how to order wine on a date or which fork to use. While these niceties are important, they're not what *The Rules* focus on. *The Rules* are about saving women—and men, for that matter—heartache. There are many disastrous relationships out there because women either initiated relationships with men or kept them going long after they should have been over. A failed relationship is depressing, confidence-shaking, and altogether unpleasant. By following *The Rules*, you avoid these disastrous results—and these painful emotions.

We had to write *The Rules* strictly, like a strict diet book, because we knew women would break them. You always sneak in your favorite high-fat meal or a piece of chocolate cake on Saturday night. With such strict rules, even if women broke the occasional rule, they could still reap the benefits of doing the rest.

Even therapists, whom we were sure would find the "be mysterious" part of *The Rules* objectionable, are actually recommending the book to their clients (see Chapter 8). They agree that the openness and honesty so necessary in therapy do not work in the initial stages of dating.

Are *The Rules* too marriage-minded? No, just realistic. Many women want to get married, and why not? It's great to have a wonderful man to share your life with—end of story. We're not telling women they're nothing without a man. It's just that many women feel that if they don't marry a nice guy, they're missing something. It's a fact. This is how they really feel. It's not a moral issue. Can they be happy without a husband? Sure. Can you be happy without taking vacations? Sure, but why would you want to?

We are not advocating marriage at any cost. On the contrary, in Chapter 17, "Buyer Beware," we explain how to determine if he's Mr. Right. This is a thinking woman's guide to marriage. This is not about being a Stepford wife.

Indeed, *The Rules* represents a change in attitude about dating, a new spirituality that is sorely needed today. It's going against nature when you chase a man, sleep with him too soon, or beg him to marry you. He may end up mistreating you, even if he marries you. He may never forgive you for trapping him and treat you badly.

Conversely, when you do *The Rules* on a man who initially showed interest, he gets to fall in love with you and value you. He does not take you for granted. Every phone call and date is precious. He never feels trapped or that you pressured him to marry you because *he* did the calling, the pursuing, the proposing.

*Rules* marriages are happy marriages. *Rules* husbands make wonderful partners for life. They are attentive and involved husbands and fathers. They change diapers, help the kids with their homework, and plan family vacations.

*The Rules* work. They really do. That's why women who want to be happily married—or at the very least, in a loving relationship—are living by *The Rules*—and loving the results!

# Chapter 2 _____

# *Rules* for Turning a Friend Into a Boyfriend

Y ou've been friends for ages. Now, for whatever reason, you've decided he's The One. Can you turn a friend into a boyfriend?

Only if *he* really always liked you, but you or circumstances prevented the friendship from developing further. For example, *you* never wanted anything more until recently, or you were both dating other people. Maybe you couldn't imagine him as a boyfriend because of age differences (he's much older or younger than you), personality differences (he's artsy, you're a business-type), or you come from different backgrounds.

How can you be sure he always liked you as more than a friend if you've just been friends?

There are certain things a friend does or says when he is drawn to you. For example:

He always just happens to be in your neighborhood or business area. He likes to watch *Friends* in your apartment. He likes your TV set better. If you are coworkers, he's frequently drinking water from the fountain near your desk. If you're in college, he's always hanging out outside of your dorm room or is often at the dining hall when you're there.

The bottom line: when a man is attracted to you, he finds ways—excuses—to be near you. We're not exaggerating when we say, whoever's near you likes you! You don't have to look far or wide to find him. He's always hanging around. You can't get rid of him!

When a friend wants to date you, he doesn't talk about other women, even if he's dating someone else. He never seems to notice other women, even your very attractive friend. If, in fact, he is attracted to other women, he tells everyone but you. Around you, the words will just not come out, they stick in his throat.

While he's private about his own love life, he wants to know about yours and asks a lot of questions. He wants to know the type of guy you like to date and what you like to do on Saturday night. He makes it sound as if he's just curious, *no big deal, of course,* but he's really figuring out how he's going to use that information to make a move one day. He thinks anyone you're dating is not good enough for you. He'll even put them down ("His father got him the job.").

When a male friend is really interested in you, he tries to be helpful. He offers to show you how to play tennis or how to work the computer. He might help you move your stuff from one apartment to another or listen to your work or roommate problems without expecting anything in return. In fact, he never expects you to help him with anything, unless it's an excuse to stay connected to you.

If he likes you as more than a friend, he'll tease you, flirt with you, and make you laugh. He thinks your shortcomings are cute.

He means more than he says. He tries to be cool around you, but he's really quite nervous.

When a male friend is *not* interested in you romantically, he behaves quite differently. He's calm, rational, matter-of-fact. You can take everything he does and says at face value.

He asks you for advice about dating another woman because he *really* wants your advice! He's simply interested in a woman's perspective. He's not secretly in love with you or bringing it up to get closer to you. He talks freely about liking other women. He might even say in front of you, "She's really cute." He doesn't think he could be hurting your feelings because you're his friend. You're like his sister—there's no sexual undercurrent.

When a male friend likes you as a friend, he's not that interested in your love life. He's satisfied with your friendship. If you're not dating anyone, he might offer to fix you up with someone, but he doesn't want to go out with you himself. He doesn't want to start anything, he feels no spark.

If you're having a problem with the guy you're dating, he will try to help you "work it out," as opposed to helping you get out of the relationship! He's not angry if he sees you with other men because he's not interested in you romantically. He *wants* to see you happy. If he's a little jealous when you have a boyfriend, it's in the same way a close girlfriend might be. Your relationship reminds him of what he doesn't have and takes time away from your friendship with him. It's a friendship loss, not a romantic loss. This, however, doesn't mean he wants you. You'd know if he did—if you thought about it honestly or read this chapter.

When a male friend is just a friend, he helps you as much as you help him. He'll show you how to read a financial statement, you'll teach him how to cook. Everything's dutch treat. It's a mutually beneficial relationship.

A male friend might even be your best friend—someone who would be there in a pinch if you ever needed him. He would lend you money to pay your rent, visit you in the hospital if you had an accident, or come to the funeral if a family member died. *But he doesn't look down the street when you walk away, try to stare at you when you're not looking, or secretly dream about having sex with you. And such feelings on a man's part are essential in the beginning of a romantic relationship!*

If he likes you only as a friend, there is nothing you can do about becoming his girlfriend. Don't try to convince him by having a heart-to-heart talk about your feelings because it will probably put a strain on your friendship. He will feel awkward or sorry for you, but he still won't feel a spark. He may try a "let's sleep together" once or twice. But it won't mean much to him and you, if not both of you, will come to regret it.

Worse yet, the two of you may decide to date or even get married at *your* initiation. But because *he* never felt a spark, your marriage will be more of a friendship and if you want more than that you will constantly be unhappy. You will be doubting your looks and your sexuality and complain, "He never notices me." Your self-confidence really plummets when you sleep with or get involved with a man who only really wanted a friendship. It's a bad road to travel. Don't even try it.

Just do *The Rules*—not to get him to like you since you can't—but for *your* self-esteem. Do *The Rules* so that your whole life isn't about this unavailable friend. Don't call him. When he calls, get off the phone in ten minutes. Don't play therapist when he talks about his girlfriend problems. More important, try to meet other men. You're better off forcing yourself to go to social events to meet your possible husband than forcing yourself on this friend.

But if you think he may be interested in you, you can casually mention that you're having boyfriend problems, not seeing your boyfriend anymore or that you're not dating anyone in particular. See how he reacts. If he's interested, he'll ask you out, and then start doing *The Rules*.

Don't talk to him like a friend—like Elaine on *Seinfeld*—but be light, feminine, and mysterious. Don't tell him all your problems. Don't start pursuing him with calls, notes, and dinner invitations. Don't think you can say or do anything you want—call him whenever you feel like it or suddenly try to increase the time you spend together—because you were platonic friends. Concentrate on making your relationship a *Rules* relationship. Keep in mind, the dynamics will be a little different now. For example, if he's from out-of-town and used to crashing on your couch when he visits you, now you should be the first to say, "It's been great, but I have a really big day tomorrow," and end the evenings first.

Now that you want him, you may be tempted to go to the other extreme—call him all the time, talk about your change of heart, refer to him as your soul mate, talk about marriage or the future—and drive him away. Men don't like to be overwhelmed, *even by women they like.*

Many women who wake up one day and decide that their male friend is their soul mate have been known to come on too strong and overwhelm their friend. Remember, part of the reason he liked you is that you didn't really notice him, and never pursued him! You've been a challenge—not because you were trying to do *The Rules*—but because you were truly not interested. You were naturally indifferent.

Therefore, when you start to date, you must not let the fact that he always liked you stop you from doing certain rules. For example, don't see him at the last minute or all the time. Don't start knitting him sweaters or talk about marriage or moving in. Okay, you've decided he's The One. But until he's decided you're The One and courts you and proposes, you have to do *The Rules*—or you might ruin a good thing!

# *Chapter 3* _____

# Second Chances—*Rules* for Getting Back an Ex

I f you are someone who read *The Rules* and thought, "If only I had done *The Rules* on my old boyfriend" or "So that's why he wouldn't commit!" then this chapter is for you.

You may not have seen him in months or even years, but now you're convinced he could have been The One. You didn't know any better and you blew it . . . and now you could kick yourself! If only you had known *The Rules* back then!

You want him back. At the very least, you want to give the relationship a second chance. You want to do *The Rules* this time and see what happens. You're wondering if there's any hope. You want to know what to do next, if anything.

Before you make a move, take a deep breath, calm down, and forgive yourself. Realize that what you're going through is very common—regretting the past,

19

wishing you had behaved differently with a certain man, thinking he's the one that got away and you'll never meet anyone better. We've received hundreds of letters from women that begin with: "I wish I had had this book ten years ago when I was dating (fill in the blank)." These women either just didn't know they should behave a certain way with men, or they instinctively knew they should but didn't have the strength to do it without specific guidelines and support.

Of course all you care about now that you've read *The Rules* is, can you get him back?

It depends.

If you initiated the relationship—spoke to him first, asked him out—and he eventually ended it, then it's not only over, *it was never meant to be.* Don't call him or write him or try to contact him in any way to say you've changed and want a second chance. He didn't really want you in the first place. Forget him and move on!

But if he pursued you and you broke rules—for example, you were possessive, saw him every night, or moved in with him and he broke it off because he felt suffocated—there may be hope. There's one way to find out and we call it "One Call for Closure."

Call him *once* when you're sure he's not home, so you get his answering machine. Calling when he's not in is crucial; you don't want to make him uncomfortable if he doesn't want to hear from you or is involved with someone else or even married. Leaving a message also allows him to call you if and when *he* wants to, which is the best start for any conversation between you. Your message gives him time to think and the option of not calling, which you must give him. Of course, if his answering machine says, "We're not home right now" and you hear a woman's voice chiming in, do not leave a message. Leave him alone and go on with your life.

Assuming he's not involved with someone, we suggest you leave the following message: "Hi, it's (your name). I just wanted to say hello, to see how you're doing. You can reach me at (phone number)." That's it!

If you don't hear from him, it's over. Don't call again to make sure he got the message. He got the message. His answering machine isn't broken. Don't write him or track him down at work, home, his favorite bar, or the gym. That's called stalking. Forget all about him and move on. You must work on accepting the way he feels and not dwelling on the past and what might have been. Don't berate yourself; if you were supposed to end up with him, you would have. Tell yourself there's someone else out there for you, try to date others, and keep doing *The Rules.*

If he does call, don't automatically assume he's rekindling the romance. He might just be returning your call, being polite, nothing deep. So try not to get too excited or show how happy you are to hear from him. Be cool, cordial. Say, "Oh hi. How are you?" Don't say, "I was hoping you'd call."

If he asks why you called, just say, "Oh, I just wondered how you were doing and wanted to say hello." Keep the conversation light . . . business, vacations, and so on. Don't ask him if he ever thinks about you or misses you, if he's seeing anyone new. After ten minutes, say, "Well, I have to get going. It was nice talking to you." Don't stay on the phone for thirty minutes or an hour, waiting and hoping he will suggest drinks. If he doesn't ask you out within ten minutes, he's not interested. Remember, if he is interested but needs more than ten minutes to ask out an ex-girlfriend, he can always call you again!

If he does ask you out, say yes if it's for a future date—it need not be a Saturday night the first time you meet, but it should be at least three days in advance. You want to let him know that your life didn't stop since the two of you split and that your calendar is full.

Your first date with an ex-boyfriend is very much like a first date with a man you just met. It's almost like a new relationship, so let him pick you up and take you out.

Look very, very good when you meet him. Extra care with your makeup, pretty outfit. Don't dress down as if it's your 200th date, even if technically, it is. Be light, casual, upbeat. Needless to say, don't have a heavy discussion about your relationship or the past, unless he brings up the subject. Even if he talks about the way it was, try not to dwell on it. Discuss general topics such as what you have both been doing professionally, if he still runs three miles every morning, and so on. Keep the date on a "let's catch up" level, as opposed to "what you've been through since the breakup" level. By the way, you should not tell him how much or how little you've dated since the breakup. Be honest, but mysterious.

Don't get terribly serious. Don't tell him that you now realize all the mistakes you've made since the relationship with him ended and how much you've changed and how you want another chance. It's too intense. Besides, it's easy to tell someone how much you've changed. The important part is actually *being* a changed person when he dates you!

Don't tell him that you've read *The Rules* and now realize what you did wrong—that you were too needy, that you shouldn't have gotten mad when he went out with the guys, and that you'll never be that way again. Simply be light. Try to be the girl he originally fell in love with.

End the date first.

Don't go back to his apartment or invite him up to yours or even think of having sex with him that night. *Remember, this is a first date. If anything, you must be extra strict with this man. He dumped you once, he can hurt you again.*

If this is to be a *Rules* relationship, he must call you and ask you out for Saturday night from now on. Seeing you either awakened a desire to date you again and to renew the relationship, or it didn't. The only way to find out is if he calls you and asks you out. You should not ask him if he missed you or if he wants to get back together. If he is to pursue you, he should not know exactly how you feel about him. He should think, "She called me one day. She might be interested, but I'm not sure. Maybe she was just bored or found an old photo of us." Remain mysterious—if he thinks that you've decided he's The One, he could get scared.

If he calls, you must do all *The Rules* outlined in our first book, specifically, "How to Act on Dates 1, 2, and 3" and "How to Act on Dates 4 through Commitment Time." Treat him like a new boyfriend—don't talk about the past or act too chummy. For example, you should not call his family, even if you met his parents and sister twenty times when you were dating. Remember, you've been apart. He has to invite you to any social events with his family and friends all over again.

If you meet him for dinner and he never calls again, he may not have felt a strong enough spark. Maybe he thought about it, but never got around to picking up the phone. Men can be that way. Maybe he's involved with someone else, but didn't tell you and met you for old time's sake.

We know of several women who contacted old boyfriends for various reasons—to make amends for the past, to discuss a business problem, or to try to start over. In each case, these men met them for drinks, said they had a great time and hoped they could stay good friends, and then never called again.

We can only say that if this happens to you, you must try to accept that it's over for him and move on.

Now what if this man happens to be your ex-husband and you've decided you want him back?

Again, it depends. If *he* initiated the divorce, you can make "One Call for Closure" and then follow the plan (outlined above) for getting back an ex-boyfriend. But don't start making room in your closet. When a man initiates a divorce, he's usually gone! It's over and out.

However, if *you* initiated the divorce but are now sorry and miss him, there is hope, especially if you are still in contact with your ex and sense that he would be open to a reconciliation—maybe you have kids together and he lingers a while when he comes by on weekends to pick them up or just seems to find reasons to call you, to be friends, to be in your life. But you're wondering, how do you go about telling him you want him back without making a fool of yourself or risking rejection?

We suggest you simply weave the following question into a friendly conversation the next time you see him or he calls: "Have you ever had second thoughts about our divorce?" *That's it. Don't say another word.* Don't get sentimental and weepy and pour your heart out. He must take it from there, give you some indication that he would also like a reconciliation, whether it be then or at some point in the future when he's had a chance to sort it out. Whatever you do, don't rush him. Let him proceed at his own pace. He may suggest having dinner or drinks to talk things over, but these must be his overtures. You've done your part. Now it's up to *him*.

We've outlined our suggestions for getting back an ex. But don't be too upset if your old boyfriend or ex-husband just won't come back. Remember, there was a reason the relationship didn't work out before, so don't romanticize it. Also, comfort yourself with the knowledge that it's usually easier to do *The Rules* on a new man than an ex.

Sometimes trying to rekindle an old flame works, but frequently the best advice we can give a woman who thinks she's still in love with her ex is *Next!*

## Chapter 4

# Don't Waste Time on Fantasy Relationships

If you have a good rapport with your doctor, lawyer, or accountant, you may find yourself wondering if he is interested in you romantically. You're not alone, but you may not be seeing the situation for what it is. How can you know for sure? It's simple. Has he ever asked you out? Has he ever suggested having a drink, coffee, lunch, or dinner? If the answer is no, then he's not!

This may sound obvious, but you'd be surprised how many women tell themselves it's romance when a man pays them the slightest attention out of professional courtesy. We wrote this chapter to smash any delusions you might have about a fantasy relationship of your own. Unless he asks to spend time with you in a nonprofessional capacity, a relationship beyond business does not exist—and *Rules* girls don't waste their time on nonexistent relationships!

The fact is, when a man is interested in a woman—including a female patient or client, employer or employee—he finds some way to ask her out. He may invite her to work out at his gym, attend a fund-raiser with him, or to play tennis over the weekend. He may not necessarily ask her out for a Saturday night date since that might be too obvious, or awkward, or forward, but he'll figure out some way to see her outside of the office. This behavior is different from the professional courtesy of a physician or financial advisor, who might say, "Call me anytime," which women mistakenly interpret as romantic interest.

Let's examine three fantasy relationships and *The Rules's* answers to remove any doubt you might have about a similar situation in your life.

**Fantasy Relationship #1:** Your internist of two years told you "beep me anytime" if your asthma acts up. He once told you to call him by his first name. He puts his arm around your shoulders when he escorts you out of his office. You just know he would ask you out if you weren't his patient. And, naturally, you want to have a "talk" with him or ask him out!

*The Rules* answer: If a doctor is friendly, affectionate, concerned, and kind, then he's doing his job. It's not a come-on for a doctor to tell a patient to beep him or call the office "day or night" if his patient has asthma—people can die of asthma, and it's his job to make sure his patients stay alive and well. Some doctors are informal (it's okay to call them by their first name) and others are touchy-feely (they kiss *all* their patients hello and good-bye). It's just good bedside manners—and good business—for a doctor to show warmth and caring. If he were romantically interested in you and uncomfortable about dating a patient, he would refer you to his associate and then ask you out.

Sure, it's a little more complicated for a doctor, lawyer, or CEO to pursue a patient, client, or associate. But it's not impossible. We've heard about bosses who've dated and even married their employees, even though it was frowned upon by the company. At first they kept the relationship a secret and then they voluntarily decided he or she would transfer to another division or another company so they could date freely.

**Fantasy Relationship #2:** Your accountant called you over the weekend to remind you to send in your tax forms before April 15. You think because he called you on Saturday at home instead of during the week at work there might be something there.

*The Rules* answer: Accountants work on the weekends, especially during the busy tax season. The lines between work and home, during-the-week, and weekends can be very blurry in business. Unless he suggested brunch, don't read into it.

**Fantasy Relationship #3:** You think the waiter at the restaurant you go to twice a week likes you because he always remembers how you like your eggs and that you take your coffee light with two sugars. You think he's more attentive to you than other customers—refills your coffee before you ask—and always makes conversation with you. You want to let him know you're not seeing anyone seriously and would go out with him if he asked. The problem is, he hasn't. What to do?

*The Rules* answer: Waiters are in the service business. It's normal for a waiter to remember a regular customer's preferences. He works for tips so it's in his interest to be friendly, make conversation, get your order right. If he liked you beyond this, however, he would suggest having drinks one night.

The point bears repeating: When a man is really interested in a woman, he figures out some way to ask her out.

Don't be insulted. We're not suggesting that your doctor, broker, or accountant isn't fond of you, just that it's not a *Rules* relationship until he asks you out.

Also keep in mind that many men, including professionals, like to flirt with women. Looking at lab results, contracts, and financial statements all day can get pretty boring, so it's fun for them to make small talk, notice your figure if you're in good shape, and compliment you on your new hairstyle. After all, they are men and they do like to look at women! It's also an ego boost for them to put on the charm, knowing that it gives some of their female patients/clients high school girl crushes. But it's all quite harmless, so don't take it seriously unless he asks you on a date.

We're not saying that you can't daydream about your sexy doctor or look forward to quarterly meetings with your handsome financial planner. Being a *Rules* girl doesn't mean you can't have obsessions, it means you don't act on them.

The danger lies in thinking there's a relationship there,

and not being open to real relationships. Women who are absorbed in fantasy relationships usually don't have real ones!

Ask yourself, are you doing everything to meet men or are you living for the day when your dream lover asks you out? You're less likely to place a personal ad, sign up with a dating service, or take that singles ski trip if you believe you're in a relationship.

Remember, *Rules* girls know they're either dating a man or not. There's nothing in between.

So if you thought your broker or lawyer was interested in you, but after reading this chapter realize he may like you but not romantically, try to accept the truth instead of fighting it. Your first impulse may be to clear the air, be open and honest—ask him if he has feelings for you but isn't acting on them because of your professional relationship. You might want to write him a note or, worse, a long letter explaining how you feel.

Don't. First, that's not *The Rules*. He must initiate any such talk. Second, nothing good will come of it. If you talk to him and he tells you that you misread his politeness and that he's just as nice to every other client/patient, you'll feel foolish and hurt—not to mention embarrassed about seeing him again professionally.

If, on the other hand, he tells you he is attracted to you, but has decided not to pursue the relationship because he's involved with someone else or more interested in you as a client/patient than a lover, you're not much better off. You have the ego satisfaction of knowing that he's attracted to you, but so what? You still don't have a Saturday night date, much less a relationship. And it's a hollow victory anyway because if he was really *crazy* about you—and why would a *Rules* girl settle for anything less?—he would rather date you than just have a professional relationship with you.

So if you can't tell him how you feel, what can you do? *The Rules.* Look your best whenever you see him, end all phone calls/meetings first, show no interest in him personally, don't send him holiday cards (if you mistakenly thought that would make him think about you in a different light) or invite him to your New Year's party to pave the way from a professional relationship to a social one. Don't buy him a tie for Christmas or bake him cookies for the holidays. Gifts don't make men think about women or ask them out. Try to treat him as you would an elderly or unattractive man—not the handsome hunk you think he is!—someone you wouldn't think twice about, much less bake brownies for!

Doing *The Rules* won't make him ask you out if he was never going to, but it will keep you from wasting time baking cookies and writing notes to men who aren't interested in you. You'll have more self-esteem.

Of course, the best thing you can do is try to meet other men, *men who do ask you out.* Nothing replaces a fantasy relationship better than a *Rules* one! So move on!

## Chapter 5

# Don't Stand by His Desk and Other *Rules* for the Office Romance

The office is one of the trickiest places to follow *The Rules* because if you are dating someone at work, your professional life and your love life may overlap to some extent. Therefore, you must do *The Rules* strictly so you don't place your job or your relationship (or both) in jeopardy.

Of course, the first rule is to figure out whether or not you are actually *in* an office romance. A lot of men like to flirt with women at the office. They don't think twice about it, it means nothing to them and it should mean nothing to you! (See Chapter 4: "Don't Waste Time on Fantasy Relationships.")

If you have a crush on someone in your office—a coworker, employee, or your boss—and he's never asked you out, don't try to get his attention. Some dating books have suggested you drink from the water cooler near his office or use the copier closest to his desk or even ask him out to lunch to discuss business. *The Rules* say, do your job and look your best. Don't look for excuses to talk to him or walk by his desk. (You shouldn't have to do any of these things to make him notice you. He either notices you or he doesn't!)

Don't tell yourself that he would have asked you out if you didn't work for the same company. There are enough office romances out there to refute that theory. As we have stated, if it is not a company code, bosses have no problem dating employees and even their own secretaries if they want to. On the other hand, don't count on working for the same company to be the spark that will unite you. Don't stay at the company hoping that one day he will notice you and ask you out. We know women who waited in vain for years for that to happen. *Rules* girls don't hold themselves back for a fantasy relationship.

Now assuming you are dating a coworker or even your boss, how should you act? Below are fourteen rules for office dating. Do them to the letter because you might have to see this man on a daily basis. There's nothing worse than having to work with a man you dread seeing or who dreads seeing you everyday because you broke rules—or working with him after he drops you! These rules are not just good for the relationship, but for your company and your career. You'll be a better worker if you're not figuring out ways to be with him all day!

1. Do not go to work everyday, motivated by the prospect of seeing him or spending time with him, or you might act out on your feelings. Go to work

33

thinking, how can I work hard today and contribute to my company—or at the very least, how can I not break *The Rules*. Try to be busy, as opposed to daydreaming at your desk or, worse, finding reasons to talk to him or see him. (When the urge to stop by his office hits you, begin a new project or stop by a friend's desk to say hello.) If he stops by your desk, be nice, but end the conversation after five or ten minutes unless it's business-related. Just pick up the papers on your desk and say, "I'd better get back to work!"

2. Work hard, but don't be such a tireless worker that you don't care about your appearance. Don't spend so much time at the office that you have no time for such mundane tasks as taking your clothes to the dry cleaner or getting a manicure. We know women who are smart and attractive, but you can't help but notice the coffee stains on their blazers, their scruffy shoes, and untweezed eyebrows. Don't be like that. You're a *Rules* girl!

Make sure you're wearing fashionable suits and shoes—you want to look as good as you can! Don't wear pantyhose with runs in them—keep extra pairs in your desk drawer in case they rip at work. Shine your shoes. Wear makeup and perfume, but not too much. (It's an office, not a disco!) Remember, you're a creature unlike any other and you care about your looks. Do all of this for yourself, but also because you could run into him or someone else at the office.

3. Do not agree to see him on a moment's notice just because you work together. If he stops by your desk and casually asks you to have lunch with him that day or to have drinks after work that evening, say you'd love to, but can't. Even if you are free for lunch or drinks, don't see him on short notice. He should be asking you out in advance for the weekend.

   If you see him on a whim, the relationship will become too casual. He won't think you're special enough to plan in advance to see you. In addition, if you allow the relationship to be on a coworker level, it could take him years to propose. We know a very attractive woman who accepted last-minute dates from a man she worked with. Several times a week at 6:00 P.M. he would drop by her desk and suggest having drinks. She always said yes. He also couldn't commit to Saturday night dates until Friday or Saturday because he "wasn't sure what *he* was doing." She accepted his behavior because she didn't know there was a better way. It took him six years to propose and their marriage is troubled; he never seems to really make the effort, and she feels taken for granted.

   So, just because you work at the same company doesn't mean he can see you whenever he feels like it. Don't make it so easy for him. He has to ask you out in advance—otherwise, you're busy! If you work closely together, you should sometimes disappear at lunch hour. Don't tell him where you're going. Remember, he works with you and dates you—that can get a little all-consuming, so you must be doubly careful to remain a little mysterious!

4. Be discreet. Don't talk about the relationship with coworkers. If anyone asks you what you did over the weekend, don't say, "David and I went hiking." Just say that *you* went hiking. Don't answer any questions with "we." It may hurt your career to be the subject of office gossip. It's not good for the relationship, either, since no man likes to date a big mouth. Men love privacy. Anything coworkers know about the relationship should come from him!

   Likewise, don't volunteer information to him. For example, don't tell him where you're going on a business trip or who you're having a meeting with unless he specifically asks about either.

5. If you need to talk to the man you are dating about business—perhaps he's your boss—by all means, talk to him! Always be professional and return his calls promptly if it is a business matter. Just check your motives. Is it really necessary to contact him, or are you looking for an excuse to be with him? For example, don't knock on his door to tell him about concert tickets or a lecture on personal growth! If it is work-related, keep the conversation brief and end it first.

   If possible, leave the information with his secretary or in his "in box." Write any memos or notes in a businesslike manner. Do not leave love notes or cute Post-it's on his desk. If he needs to talk to you, he can always come to *your* office or leave you a note!

6. He can E-mail you as much as he wants, but don't E-mail him back every time unless it is business-related. On all nonbusiness E-mails, once for every four of his E-mails is a good rule of thumb. Remember, keep your E-mails brief and breezy and stick to business. This is important, because you never know who has access to your E-mail—it may be read by the head of the company, so keep all romance off the screen and save it for Saturday nights.

7. Don't snoop around his office. You shouldn't even be near his office! Don't ask his secretary who calls him or who he's having lunch with and where. It's none of your business. Besides, she might tell him and he will be annoyed and resent it.

8. Don't make your office a shrine to your relationship. Don't put his photo in a frame on your desk or keep the teddy bear he gave you for Valentine's Day in your office after February 14. It's best to be businesslike.

Speaking of your office, be neat. Neat is sexy. No one likes to date a slob. So don't be a pack rat. Don't have piles of paper on your desk or stash half-eaten sandwiches in your desk drawer. Don't collect objects or hang memorabilia on the walls. Don't decorate your office like a college dorm room. Don't be cute or juvenile. Be professional.

9. Don't kiss or hold hands at the office. Not only is it unprofessional, it's not good for *The Rules*. He has to ask you out on a date to kiss you or spend quality time with you. Don't agree to go to a hotel with him during your lunch hour. That's not a date and he won't respect you (and you'll come back from lunch looking rumpled and unbusinesslike). No one wants a reputation—be careful that you don't earn one. Again, he has to ask you out for the weekend for you to take dating him seriously!

10. Don't sleep with your boss or coworker unless you're in a committed relationship—not just for sex and not to further your career. Bad motives tend to backfire.

   Keep in mind that *The Rules* don't stop because you're out of town. If you're on a business trip together and it would be easy to have sex because you're staying at the same hotel—still say no if you're not in a committed relationship. It may seem tempting—you are away from the office, and who will know? But remember, eventually you have to return home—back to reality—and you'll regret sleeping with him if he isn't serious about you or ignores you when you return to the office.

11. Don't hang out at the office at the end of the day or go to happy hour with the gang after work. You do not want to be thought of as the office party girl, but the kind of girl men marry. And of course don't get drunk at the office Christmas party or at any other party. It's hard to do *The Rules* when you're drunk!

12. If you work in different cities for the same company, let him travel to visit you three times before you visit him. If you're sent to his city on business, don't mention getting together. *He* must suggest making plans. If things do get serious, you shouldn't relocate until you have a commitment/wedding date.

13. Don't stay at the company just because he works there. If you are not happy with your job or are interested in other opportunities, pursue them. We don't hold ourselves back for a man. If it's good for your career to leave the company, go! Doing what's good for you will also show him you're independent, not clingy. It might make him miss you and propose faster because he can't see you everyday.

14. Do not suggest commuting together even if you live near each other and work at the same company. It must be his suggestion and you should turn him down sometimes just so he doesn't take you for granted and so you can remain mysterious.

Married women have written to us asking how they should behave if they work with their husbands.

We hope they were either already working together when they met, or that it was their husband's idea to work together. Women should never suggest working with their husbands as a way of spending more time with them or checking up on them. It's not *The Rules,* and men hate it. You should only work with your husband if there is a legitimate reason to and/or it was his idea.

Regardless of why you are working together, here are five rules:

1. Do not suggest sharing an office or putting your desks near each other. Any togetherness must come from him.
2. Do not be the one to suggest commuting together.
3. Do not suggest having lunch together. You both need some time apart during the day.
4. Don't spy on him, don't ask his secretary who called, or get upset if he talks to other women.
5. Don't bring up personal business at the office and discourage him if he does. Be professional. Do your job!

## Chapter 6

# Long-Distance Relationships.
# Part I: How They Should Start

$M$any questions arise in long-distance relationships that don't come up when dating a man closer to home. But before going into the specific rules for these relationships, it's important to talk about the mistakes women make when they first meet a man from out-of-town—mistakes that can easily prevent a long-distance *Rules* relationship from ever developing. As we have said before, it's the first encounter—who spoke to whom first, how long the conversation lasted, and who ended it first—that often determines whether it's a *Rules* relationship or not.

Let's look at some typical scenarios:

You meet a man at a mutual friend's wedding in Atlanta. You're from New York and he's from Chicago. He comes up to you and asks you to dance. It's *The Rules*! You like him a lot. You dance one dance and then another and then another. You feel glued to his side.

You know you should really walk away, say hello to

41

some college friends you haven't talked to in years, but you don't. You figure the two of you live miles apart, who knows if you'll ever see him again, so what's the harm with spending five hours with him?

He asks you to join him for dessert. You say yes. Then he invites you to take a walk with him around the grounds. You agree. He takes your phone number at the end of the evening, kisses you good-bye, and says something about calling you in a few days, maybe visiting New York.

You're in love. You fly back home and tell your friends and your mother, and start thinking about your *own* wedding.

But because you broke *The Rules* by spending so much time with him, he either never calls, or calls after a week or two just to say hello but doesn't make plans to see you. Or he calls and asks you to fly to Chicago to see him, or makes plans to see you in New York but only because he's going to be there on business anyway. Naturally, you feel hurt and disappointed. Why doesn't he sound crazy about you? Why doesn't he want to jump on a plane and see you right away?

Looking back on the evening—and after reading *The Rules*—you realize that you didn't play hard to get. You spent five straight hours with him. He knew you liked him and the challenge was gone.

We're not saying that had you walked away or turned him down a couple of times for dances that he would definitely call and pursue a long-distance relationship. Maybe he has a girlfriend in Chicago, maybe he just wanted to have fun at the wedding—nothing more, nothing less.

But by *not* doing *The Rules,* you lessened your chances, you got your hopes up, and you got emotionally involved and hurt. If he was interested and you were more elusive, chances are he would have thought about you on the plane ride home, missed you in Chicago, called sooner, and made plans to see you in New York, even if he didn't have a business trip there.

In the future, when you meet someone at a wedding or party whom you may never see again, don't spend the entire evening with him. Talk to him for fifteen to twenty minutes, dance with him a couple of times, and then excuse yourself to use the ladies' room or say hello to a friend or just walk around for a while. He should be looking for you during the evening and trying to pin you down for another dance.

When you spend four or five hours with a man you just met, he no longer finds you as mysterious or interesting, even if he made the first move. When he goes back home, he may not think you're that special or dream about seeing you again because you were too available.

The same goes for meeting a man on a business trip. Let's say you meet a man at a conference. He notices you, strikes up a conversation, and asks you to have dinner with him that evening since he's leaving town the next morning. You say yes because he's cute and maybe something will start. You tell yourself you may never cross paths again—he's from Boston and you're from San

Diego—and you weren't going to do anything special for dinner anyway but order room service and HBO.

*The Rules* answer is to say, "Thank you, but I already have plans." Why? Because if you see him at the last minute, even if it's convenient for both of you, some of the challenge evaporates. If he's interested in you, let him call you and make special plans to visit you. If he can see you at a moment's notice, he won't have to long for you and pursue you and whatever interest he had in you may fizzle.

Don't think we're being overly strict about this. We see it happen time and time again. A woman meets a man at a business function or a party who says he's in town for just a few days and wants to take her to dinner that very night. He's totally charming and makes her feel special. She tells herself that she would really be missing something if she turned him down. He won't be in town again for another month.

He's a sexy movie producer or a plastic surgeon with offices on both coasts. She says yes—maybe it's just dinner, maybe she sleeps with him—and she thinks this is the beginning of a whirlwind bicoastal courtship.

The reality is, it may not be. He may be lying. He may be in town for another week, but figures this way he'll get what he wants right away. Or he may be married and this is his standard pickup line when he's out of town. There are men who have a girl in every port. You don't want to be one of them. But even if he's sincere, single, and really likes you, the answer is still no to a last-minute date. You think if you say no, he'll forget you. But *Rules* girls know that he'll remember you that much more if you turn him down.

So the next time you meet a man who asks you to dinner the same night because he's in town just a few days, say, "I'd love to, but I have other plans." Let him call you in advance the next time he plans to be in town or make a special trip to see you.

The only way to know if a man is really interested in you—instead of just filling up a few hours—is to not accept a last-minute date. When you make him wait several days to see you or you make him wait until he's in town again a month later, he gets to experience longing. If his feelings about you are just lukewarm, he won't bother to make a date beforehand—by following *The Rules,* you'll avoid wasting your time and having your hopes dashed later on. We know quite a few women who were full of hope, but then never heard from Mr. Bicoastal again.

Here's another common long-distance scenario. You meet Mr. Right on the first day of a seven-day vacation. Perhaps you're from different cities in the United States and you meet on a Club Med trip. He speaks to you first, asks you out for that night, and wants to be with you for all seven days and nights. You think, why not? He's cute. This is the whirlwind romance you always read about and dreamed about.

In this situation, you *must* force yourself not to see this man for the whole trip. See him once or twice for dinner and dancing over the seven-day period, but turn him down to be with other people so that he finds you mysterious and elusive and is forced to pursue you when he returns home. If he doesn't call you after the trip, at least you didn't waste seven days and nights on a man who's not that interested.

We know men who go on such trips, pursue one woman the whole time, sleep with her, and then never think about her (much less call her) again when they return home. Here, you're thinking this is true love, and he's thinking sex, sand, and fun for a week. If you don't want to be nothing more than the girl he slept with in Club Med, don't see him more than once or twice that week and don't sleep with him, otherwise you'll be crushed if you never hear from him again. It'll be a classic case of "I love you, honey, but the vacation's over."

So, by doing *The Rules,* you won't throw away a whole week on someone who may not have serious intentions, and you will be open to meeting other men. If he really likes you, he'll call you and visit you afterward.

*Chapter 7* _____

# Long-Distance Relationships.
# Part II: Making It Work

Assuming you're beginning or already in a long-distance relationship, what are *The Rules*?

You don't call him. He calls you. He can call you often, but make sure you don't spend endless hours on the phone. Leave something to talk about when he visits you! Get off the phone in fifteen to twenty minutes—you can talk longer than the standard ten minutes since it is long-distance—whether or not he talks about making plans to see you. If he wants to visit you on the weekend, he must ask you by Wednesday.

Chances are if he approached you, he'll suggest coming to visit you first, which is *The Rules*. But if he says, "Why don't you visit me in Boston? I'll show you around Cambridge," or suggests that you meet him in some city halfway, simply say, "That sounds nice, but things are really hectic right now, I just couldn't get away." Don't spell out what's hectic or exactly why you can't get away. Just say no nicely and he'll realize that he has to visit you.

If he decides not to make the trip, he didn't like you that much. Remember that men drive for hours to go to football games and gambling casinos or to their college roommate's bachelor party, so it's not a big deal if they have to drive for hours to visit you.

Better that you never see him again than you visit him first or even meet him halfway. Meeting him halfway is the same as visiting him—it's not *The Rules* to do so in the early stages of a relationship. Wait until he's visited you *three times* to visit him or meet him halfway—and even then, not too often.

Of course, some women will rationalize visiting a man first (or sooner than they should) by saying that they wanted to get away anyway—they haven't taken a vacation in years! Some reason that they have the frequent-flier miles to make the trip for free, so why not? Yes, it would be fun or free, but it's not *The Rules*!

Others convince themselves that the trip would be a great opportunity to visit a friend or relative. Please make sure you're not finding excuses to be in his city. If you do have a legitimate reason for being there—a business trip or your friend's baby shower—don't tell him about it unless he specifically asks if you're planning to be in his area anytime soon. If he does ask and you tell him your plans, don't let him assume you'll see him. He has to ask you out and come to your hotel or sister's house if he wants to see you.

If you travel to see him before he's made at least three

trips to see you, he won't think you're special, hard to see, and will not appreciate you or pursue you in the future. Even if he was initially drawn to you, he will expect you to travel to him all the time. He might start calling you at the last minute for the weekend and saying that he's too busy to leave town and suggesting that you visit him again. He might even say he's too busy to pick you up at the airport. Soon he might say he's too busy to see you at all, even though you offered to visit him. Once you start breaking *The Rules*, even promising relationships start to unravel quickly.

We've heard from women who've met multimillionaires offering to send them plane tickets or even their private jets to bring them to their homes for the weekend as a first or second date. These women are naturally flattered and excited and think the offer is special and meaningful.

We tell them it may not be and to decline very sweetly. Even if he makes $3 million a year and you're a struggling secretary, you must say, "Thank you but I just can't get away this weekend."

The reason is, he has to visit you. He has to work to see you—pack a suitcase, be inconvenienced, possibly miss the ballgame he was going to watch on TV. For a man to have his secretary call and make the arrangements requires no sweat on his part. For very little effort, he gets to have companionship and perhaps sex for the weekend. *You* have to get someone to watch your dog, experience jet lag, you have to stop your life and be inconvenienced. *Rules* girls don't turn themselves upside down for a good deal or fun weekend. They hold out for love and marriage!

So don't be blown away by a private plane, Dom Pérignon, and a limo. You might be the first woman he's met who ever said no. Don't worry. If he likes you, he'll visit you!

Assuming he is visiting you, what are *The Rules*?

For the first three times he visits you, he should not stay with you. If he asks to, say, "I don't think so. We just met." It will be up to him to find a place to stay—at a hotel or with a friend or relative. That's not your problem. Remember, the first three visits are really nothing more than three dates . . . and on the first three dates we don't have sex with a man or have him stay at our place overnight. You can invite him up on the third visit but he has to leave before the night is over. The fact that he's visiting from out-of-town doesn't change that.

Another reason not to let a man stay with you early on is to protect yourself from the type of guy who is more than happy to hop on a plane to see you, but not for the reason you think. He's just looking to have a good time in a new city with a fun girl (you!)—nothing serious. You're just part of the trip, not the main attraction. By asking him to stay in a hotel, you'll have avoided this noncommital, call-when-he's-coming-to-town type of relationship. You're not a hotel or a tourist attraction! Of course, there's nothing wrong with letting a man stay at your place as long as you can take it for what it is. But if you have dreams of love and romance, then you must do *The Rules*!

When he visits you the first three times, always see a little bit less of him than he would like. For example, if he suggests flying in Friday night and leaving Sunday evening, say Saturday morning would be better and end the weekend Sunday afternoon.

Don't cancel every single activity you normally do on the weekend so that you can be with him every minute. For example, if you have a Saturday afternoon exercise class, go to it. Let him keep himself busy and wait for you.

The point is, don't be a woman who drops everything when a man is in town. You're a *Rules* girl . . . you had a life before you met him and you still do! It's actually good for him if you have something—a previous commitment—other than him planned for that weekend. He should leave feeling that he didn't get enough of you instead of too much.

When he visits you, don't play social director. It's up to him to look into restaurants, museums, interesting places to take you or events going on that weekend. However, if he is not familiar with your town and asks you to suggest something to do, you can. But always err on the side of less. If he asks you to suggest a restaurant, do not pick out the romantic hot spot with the dim lighting and lovers' booths, but a decent place that you would take a friend or coworker. Don't try too hard to find things to do so that he's entertained and not bored. Let him pick up the newspaper or an entertainment guide and figure something out, or make plans together when he arrives. Remember, he should think you were busy and just didn't have time to think about the weekend, even if that's all you thought about all week.

Women have a tendency to think too much about the man, the weekend, and act on every thought. They make reservations at a Cajun restaurant because they remember he likes spicy food. They get two tickets to the auto show because he mentioned he was a car buff.

Your efforts might be noticed—but they'll backfire. He'll know you are intrigued and like him, that you remembered everything he ever said, and that you've been thinking about him all week and planning the perfect weekend. He'll feel smothered and you'll wonder why he stopped calling.

After he has visited you three times, you can visit him once and stay at his place, if he invites you. Who pays for the trip? It depends. If he offers to pay the airfare, let him. If he doesn't, don't ask him for the money, but let him pay for everything when you're there. Don't worry. By doing *The Rules*—visiting him infrequently—you will automatically minimize your travel costs. On the other hand, do not fly out a lot to see him just because he offers to pick up the tab. *The Rules* is about letting him pursue you, not saving money.

If you have friends or relatives in that city, it would be a good idea to call them and meet them briefly while you're there so that you don't spend the entire weekend with this man and he doesn't tire of you. End the weekend first.

Being in a long-distance relationship does not give you license to send men letters and greeting cards. You are not pen pals. You can send him a birthday or holiday card if you are in a committed long-distance relationship, assuming he sent you the same. The cards should be warm but not mushy. No love poetry.

If the relationship progresses—he's calling you every

week for the weekend, he's visiting you more than you're visiting him, he wants to be exclusive, and so on—you are in a long-distance *Rules* relationship. If this is not the case, be available to date others.

If things get serious, he might bring up the future and ask if you would ever consider relocating. Reply, "I haven't really thought about it." Until he actually proposes and gives you a ring, be vague. There is no reason to look into selling or renting your apartment or asking for a job transfer to his city or finding a job in his city if he hasn't formally proposed.

In fact, there's no reason to relocate until after you've set a wedding date. We do not live with a man before marriage, and we don't go away with him on seven-day vacations before the honeymoon. Try to see him only on the weekends until you have a wedding date.

If you are already in a long-distance relationship and did not know about *The Rules* until now, start doing *The Rules* very strictly today. Don't call him. Let him call you. Get off the phone in fifteen minutes. (Okay, twenty minutes if he's calling from Tokyo or Paris and you don't talk that often!) If he's used to you traveling to him most of the time, let him visit you more now. If he says he's too busy, simply say, "Things are so hectic . . . I just can't get away right now." This will get him to miss you, wonder about you, and figure out a way to visit you—if he's interested—and marry you!

## Chapter 8

# You *Can* Ask Your Therapist to Help You Do *The Rules*

In our first book, we told you not to discuss *The Rules* with your therapist. We felt that most therapists would not advise their patients to "play hard to get" or act contrary to their feelings. We were concerned that discussing *The Rules* in therapy would cause too much conflict. On the one hand, you have a book telling you, "Don't call him, don't tell him how you feel in the beginning of the relationship" and a therapist telling you to "Call him if you want to, tell him how you feel." We thought there would be some confusion.

We thought this because some of the women we originally helped with *The Rules* (long before it was a book) told us that it was the exact opposite of what their therapists were telling them to do with men. When they mentioned *The Rules* concept to their therapists, they were discouraged from doing them. However, when these women realized that it was *The Rules* that helped them date successfully and marry the man of their dreams, many either stopped going to therapy, or used *The Rules* for dating only and therapy for other issues.

So you can understand why we said "Don't discuss *The Rules* with your therapist." We were not trying to exclude therapists from their patients' dating process, we just didn't want women to feel torn. (After all, it's hard enough to do *The Rules* when you believe in them!)

We were pleasantly surprised to find out that a number of therapists saw our point of view. Since *The Rules* was published, we've received dozens of letters from psychotherapists and social workers saying that they agree with *The Rules* and that it gives women excellent and much needed dating guidelines and helps build their self-esteem. They are even recommending the book to their patients. Some therapists said they could never figure out why their own relationships were not working out until they read *The Rules*! Others have even started therapy groups based on *The Rules* to help women put *The Rules* into practice and overcome their resistances.

For example, one therapist told us that some of her patients feel that not returning a man's call is "rude," so she suggested they call his home number and leave a short message when he's at work. It's gratifying to know that therapists are trying to work with *The Rules*.

Therapists agree with us that such details matter. They admit that therapy has been "warm and fuzzy" about what to do and not to do, and that *The Rules* fills a void. They have come to see that *The Rules* is not just a dating book with lots of do's and don'ts, but a way of building a full life and dating with self-esteem.

According to a therapist in the Midwest, "Before *The Rules,* many women were clueless. They gave too much too soon. They got involved too quickly and then were devastated. *The Rules* takes the guesswork out of dating. It gives women boundaries. Before *The Rules,* women were unsure how much to show or give a man. Now there are no more five-hour phone conversations or visiting a man often because you're a flight attendant and it's free. Now women have to take responsibility for their actions."

This therapist has found *The Rules* particularly helpful in guiding women in the early stages of a relationship to "control their impulse to be the aggressor, to say the first word." She advises them "to let things happen."

A New York therapist also praised *The Rules* for daring to tell the truth: "You are right. Men say that they want someone who lets her needs be known, who is honest, and up front. They like women like that, they make friends with women like that, but they fall in love with and marry women who do *The Rules.* Men may say they feel *The Rules* are manipulative but they are fascinated by a woman who does them. When they are attracted to a woman they operate on the animal level . . ."

A male psychotherapist wrote to us saying that he considers *The Rules* "the definitive text on how a woman can have power with a man. It speaks very well to boundary issues which so many women struggle with these days."

Yet another therapist praised *The Rules* for articulating "the behavioral version of managing deep feelings that can get stirred up early on in romantic relationships," noting that "women are sometimes so hungry for a relationship" that they get involved emotionally and sexually too quickly and "lose out on the experience of being sought after and cherished." Therapists agree that when you do *The Rules,* you let the man pursue you and that feels great!

In defense of psychotherapy, one therapist pointed out that what goes on in sessions—the degree of honesty and openness encouraged—was never meant to be practiced on dates. That was never the intention of therapy. Perhaps therapists assumed patients would *know* they should not tell all on a date. What therapists didn't realize was that their patients were in fact sharing very deep feelings on the second or third date. Before *The Rules,* some women just didn't realize how inappropriate that was, they simply were never told *not to.*

To make our point clear, pretend you are seeing a therapist who specializes in weight loss. In the session you talk about all the feelings, frustrations, and situations that make you want to overeat. Fine. As long as when you leave his office, you don't head for the donut shop. It's the same with *The Rules.* Talk to your therapist about how you want to marry a man that you've dated twice, just don't tell *him.*

Of course, there are therapists out there who don't believe in *The Rules.* We have no interest in changing anyone's mind. We tell women, try whatever approach you like, whatever works for you. *The Rules* has worked for us and countless other women.

Assuming you believe in *The Rules* and your therapist is *not against it,* there should be no conflict between *The Rules* and therapy—as long as you do *The Rules* after you leave the therapist's office. Use therapy to talk about your feelings and dating history, discuss how you get hurt too easily, and so forth, but use *The Rules* to help you with your *dating behavior.* That means that if you feel a strong desire to call a man you just started seeing after discussing the relationship in therapy for an hour, don't call him and don't tell him on your next date how your session went. Feel your feelings, but do *The Rules.*

So if you feel your therapist can help you do *The Rules,* by all means ask him or her to help you and incorporate them into therapy.

Be careful, though, if your therapist tells you to act contrary to *The Rules.* For example, if your therapist wants you to call a man who stopped calling you in order to find out what happened/express your anger/keep the relationship going, don't. *The Rules* answer is not to call, but to tell yourself, "Good riddance, next!" If he stopped calling with no explanation, then you want nothing to do with him! You can express your anger in therapy or vent your rage on the StairMaster, but don't ask a man why he stopped calling and tell him you're angry or try to convince him to keep dating you. If he's not interested in you for whatever reason, it's nothing to be angry *at him* about. You are entitled to your anger, but calling him will seem desperate and will only make you feel worse. In addition, you don't want to *coerce* anyone to be with you!

In conclusion, the only way to know how your therapist feels about *The Rules* is to ask. So ask your therapist to help you do *The Rules*. But if he or she won't and you want to continue seeing him or her for their expertise with other issues, you probably don't need to even discuss *The Rules*. If you feel you need to discuss *The Rules* with someone, talk to *Rules*-minded women and/or join a *Rules* support group. They will provide *The Rules* help and support you need, and you won't have to do *The Rules* alone.

## Chapter 9 _____

# If He Doesn't Call, He's Not That Interested. Period!

We know this is hard to accept. We've heard it all—every rationalization imaginable used to avoid having to confront this unpleasant truth: he said he was going to call at the end of the last date, but didn't. Now you're sure it's because you didn't smile or talk enough, or you talked too much. You didn't thank him for dinner. You ordered the most expensive dish and now he thinks you're after his money.

Or he hasn't called because he's busy, or he's going through something with his father or ex-wife. Business is rough and that's why he hasn't called.

He thought you didn't have a good time on the last date, so he didn't call.

He hasn't called because he lost your number.

We can all come up with 100 reasons why a man didn't call. But the bottom line is, if he hasn't called, he's not that interested.

We're not saying he doesn't like you or that you didn't have a great date or that you're not on his mind sometimes, but if he hasn't actually dialed your number, how interested can he be?

If you have to call him to remind him you exist, something is wrong. Then, if you pursue him and he ever marries you, you'll have to remind him it's your birthday or your wedding anniversary or call him at work to get his attention. You might have to initiate sex and vacations. You'll always have to be the one to call the travel agent because he may think about vacations, but he never gets around to calling. Things are the way they are! This is not the kind of relationship a *Rules* girl wants to get involved in.

So don't waste time analyzing what you may have done to discourage him from calling. Let it go. No matter what the reason, if he doesn't call, it's next!

# 25 Reasons Why Women Want to Call Men But Shouldn't!

1. He didn't call you.
2. You think he lost your number.
3. You think he thinks you're not interested.
4. You have two tickets to a show.
5. You need a date for a wedding.
6. Your mother told you to call him.
7. Your girlfriends said, "Call him, it's the nineties."
8. Your brother said he'd be flattered if a girl called him.
9. You can't sleep well since he stopped calling.
10. You want to ask him why he stopped calling.
11. You want to get his recipe for chili.
12. You left your umbrella in his apartment.
13. You can't live without him.
14. You want to ask him what it is about you he didn't like. "Was it my hair? the sex? what was it?" You'll change whatever it was.

15. You want to know how he's doing.
16. You want to wish him a Happy Birthday or Happy New Year.
17. Your phone number is unlisted now and you want to give him your new number.
18. You're thinking about joining a convent and wanted his opinion.
19. You want to know if the new woman is thinner, prettier, smarter, better in bed, or more successful than you are.
20. You're just calling to say "hi."
21. You're never home and you're hard to reach.
22. Your answering machine is broken.
23. You're going to Paris (his favorite city) on vacation and need some sight-seeing ideas.
24. You want to ask him one more time "Is it really over?"
25. He said "Call me."

*Chapter 11* _____

# Show Up Even If You Don't Feel Like It

Some women are lucky. They marry their high school or college sweetheart at twenty-two and never have to deal with dating again. But what if that's not your story and the only man in your life is your dry cleaner? You had some relationships in the past but they didn't work out because you didn't know about *The Rules*.

There are many women in your situation. They simply never meet men. Years go by without a Saturday night date. They spend New Year's Eve with girlfriends, Chinese takeout, or a rented video.

If this is you, realize that you may not meet Mr. Right naturally and that you therefore must take social actions immediately *even if you don't want to.*

Obviously, you can't do *The Rules* if there are no men in your life. Don't despair—instead, focus on doing something—anything—to increase your chances of meeting men so you can practice *The Rules* and get married.

A good rule to start is to carry out one social action per week, *no matter what!* Here are some suggestions:

Plan to go to a singles party this weekend, get involved in a church/synagogue social event, do charity work or work on a political campaign where you might meet men, book a trip to Club Med, place a personal ad, join a dating service, take a share in a ski house, summer beach house, play tennis, jog around the park in your neighborhood, anything! You don't have to dance well, campaign well, ski well, play tennis well, or jog very far. You just have to plan these activities, show up, do your best, and smile.

Perhaps you are thinking, "But I don't have anyone to go with." Then you *must go* alone! Of course, it would be great to have a friend (with similar interests) to go with, but if you don't have one, that's no excuse to sit at home. Many women we know actually pushed themselves to go alone to a party or social affair when they absolutely didn't want to go, and those were the very nights they met their husbands.

If you keep waiting for someone to go with, a convenient ride to the event, or perfect weather, you might never go. How serious are you about meeting someone if you won't go by yourself? Sometimes it's actually *better* to go alone because you're on your own time schedule and some men might find you easier to approach.

Besides, you must learn to accept that, as an adult, you can't always rely on a friend to do things with. There are many tasks in life that have to be done alone, such as going on job interviews or going to the dentist. Some-

times you have to think about social activities as work—
you have to do them regardless of how you feel.

Motivating yourself to get off the couch, dress, put on
makeup, and show up won't be easy, but it must be done.
You may or may not have fun at the party, but at the very
least, you'll practice *The Rules* for an hour or two and go
home.

Don't think, "But I'm not comfortable" at this or that.
Go anyway!

We know it's not always comfortable to be single in social gatherings, but then again, many things we tell you
to do in *The Rules* are not always comfortable. You're also
probably worrying that the kind of men you're attracted
to won't come up to you, or that you'll be frustrated because you can't approach them since you're doing *The
Rules*. You may not feel that you will have a good time
and that you might have had more fun reading a good
book in bed, but you'll never meet anyone that way, so
you have to go!

Even if you don't meet Mr. Right, going out—whether
it be to an "in" restaurant, museum, lecture, or party—is
good for you. It's a chance to meet new people, broaden
your horizons, learn to be at ease in crowds, and best of
all, to practice *The Rules*.

Tell a friend that you're going to take one social action
this week and make sure you stick to it!

## Chapter 12

# Keep Doing *The Rules* Even When Things Are Slow

A very important *Rules* credo is that it's better to date no one than to date or marry Mr. Wrong. Better to spend Saturday night baby-sitting for your nephews or curled up with a good book than with a man who's not in love with you.

Let's say you've been doing *The Rules* for six months or even a year, but have nothing to show for it. No husband, no steady boyfriend, and few Saturday night dates. You go to parties, museums, and singles events, you look good, and you don't pursue men. Men you're attracted to don't approach you and the ones you don't care about won't leave you alone! Meanwhile, your friends who aren't doing *The Rules* seem to be dating all the time. True, their relationships aren't good—sometimes downright bad!—and don't last, but at least they're busy and you're all alone. Even your mother is telling you to call men! What's wrong with this picture?

Unfortunately, nothing. You just haven't met Mr. Right yet. The fact is, Mr. Right—the man you want to marry who wants and pursues you—only comes around a few times in a lifetime. So don't be surprised if you come home from parties with nothing good to report other than that you did *The Rules.* You didn't meet anyone. No man asked you for your number.

Many women we know went through the nothing-to-show-for-it period for a year or more, but now are happily married and glad they didn't weaken and stop doing *The Rules.*

Don't be surprised if you're tempted to break *The Rules* during these dead periods. You might long to initiate a conversation with the first cute guy you see or call an old boyfriend who didn't treat you well in an attempt to rekindle something dead and buried, just out of boredom and loneliness. We understand how you feel, but don't give in! You're just asking for heartache and wasting your time.

Realize that these dead periods are not dead at all. *The Rules* are actually working in your life because you are weeding out unsuitable men, which is just as important as holding out for Mr. Right.

When you feel that nothing is happening in the man area, take advantage of this downtime and pursue that MBA or law degree, finish the novel you started writing in college, redecorate, or find a hobby. Take up tennis or diving. Don't forget to call *Rules*-minded women or attend a *Rules* support group/seminar for reinforcement. Anything—but don't initiate a relationship with a man who isn't right for you. You never know—you might just meet your husband on the tennis court or your adult education class.

Women who break *The Rules* when nothing is going on end up in relationships that don't work out and, even worse, get involved in relationships that prevent them from meeting Mr. Right. Five months or five years later, they're still single and older. *Rules* girls don't waste time!

## Chapter 13

# Don't Tell the Media About Your Love Life and Other *Rules* for Celebrities

If you're beautiful, rich, and successful, a celebrity or the owner of your own business, you may think that you don't have to do *The Rules*. You may believe that you can get and keep a man based on your looks, money, power, or persona.

But if being rich, beautiful, famous, or powerful were enough to catch and keep Mr. Right, why are so many models, actresses, and successful businesswomen single, divorced, or in unsatisfying relationships? The answer has nothing to do with money or fame. These women are just not doing *The Rules*. They either chase men outright or don't play hard to get with men who are initially interested in them.

Actresses, models, and socialites are sometimes the worst *Rules*-breakers because they're used to men falling all over them. So they think they can even win over men who never showed any initial interest in them. Needless to say, they're wrong. The relationships they create invariably don't last, and some end up in messy public divorces.

Of course, it would help bolster our argument if we named names. However, that would hurt and embarrass the famous women involved and we would never do so. The most important lesson is to learn from these mistakes!

What's typical *Rule*-breaking behavior by an actress, model, or high-profile businesswoman? She spots a man at a party or a restaurant or a business function—if she's an actress, she may think an actor she just saw in a movie or TV commercial is really cute—and decides she wants to meet him. So she calls him up directly or has her assistant/business manager/publicist contact his assistant/business manager/publicist to make a date. If she's an actress, she may send him tickets or ask him to accompany her to a movie screening. If she's a tennis star, she may send him a VIP ticket to her next game. If she's a CEO, she may ask him to escort her to a black-tie dinner.

The man is usually flattered and agrees to go out with her. If he's attracted to her or in awe of her talent, he may date her for months or even years. He may even marry her. But in his heart he knows the relationship is not quite what he wanted. Because she wasn't someone he would have chosen on his own, there will always be something missing for him. She'll always be more interested in him than he is in her.

As time goes by, he may ignore her or even cheat on

her. Eventually, he'll leave her for someone *he noticed first and had to chase, even someone less attractive, less wealthy, or less famous.* The world may be surprised when this famous couple announces their breakup, but don't be. It was not *The Rules.*

Men want what they want. So even if you're beautiful, talented, and rich, you can't successfully pursue a man!

Far from being exempt from *The Rules,* actresses, models, high-powered, and famous women must follow *The Rules* more strictly than other women because their love life is public knowledge. If they pursue men, it will detract from their image, everyone will know about it, and they will be embarrassed.

For example, if a high-powered female executive *actively* pursues a man and then talks about the relationship with her secretary or staff, the whole company could find out about it and it could get back to him. In addition to providing fodder for the company rumor mill, the man might lose interest in her when he finds out she's too obsessed with him and that she acted indiscreetly.

If you're a famous woman and you break *The Rules,* it's even worse because you are giving men ammunition to hurt you publicly. They could inform the media and make your behavior a front-page story. They could sell love letters you wrote them to the *National Enquirer* or write a kiss-and-tell. On the other hand, when you do *The Rules,* men have nothing but good things to say about you because you left them alone. That's because the relationship—the calls, the letters, the attention, and so forth—was *their* idea. That's why we don't write men love letters or make anything happen. Why put ourselves in a position to be hurt?

In addition, by doing *The Rules,* rich and famous women can automatically weed out men who are only dating them for their fame or money. If you think nothing of inviting a man to your ski house because you have one and he doesn't, or taking a man on a vacation because you make more money than he does, remember that the trip is never as good when you invite him or pay for him. Instead, take a girlfriend, or go alone. A man might take advantage. We've heard about men who broke up with or never even called women right after these women took them on lavish vacations. Some men may accept your largesse, but then use you for it. When you do *The Rules,* you're silently letting him know that when he dates you, he gets only you—no extra perks. Unless he's interested in *you* for yourself, he drops out of the picture.

Do not use your social or business connections to help a man you are dating. If he's a lawyer and your company is looking for legal advice, don't bring him in. Think how awkward it would be if he were hired and then broke up with you! If you are wealthy, don't talk about your money or power or mention that your father is a millionaire. He should have no ulterior motives for wanting to be with you. Men should never get into the habit of expecting *anything* from you.

A wealthy woman we know who had a hard time meeting eligible men ran a personal ad in a magazine saying that she owned a large computer company, a sports car, and a ski house. She thought that her business savvy and wealth would attract interesting men—the same way some women think that giving men wild sex will keep them interested. But the men who responded to her ad showed more interest in getting a job at her company or free weekends at her ski house and country club than in dating her.

We told her to change her ad to play up her sexy smile, long hair, and great backhand. We advised her not to say anything about her business or assets in the ad or on dates until a man showed genuine interest in her. If asked about her career, we suggested she say, "I'm in management" or "I work for a computer company." We instructed her not to pick up the check on dates or invite men to her ski house. She followed our advice and is married to a man who fell for her smile and lively personality—long before he knew her net worth!

Trying to attract men with business smarts and money doesn't work. A man must feel a spark. He must like your looks and want to be with you, regardless of what you earn or own. In a *Rules* relationship, men fall in love with your essence, not your management skills.

Very wealthy women who marry men who have less money than they do should strongly consider asking them to sign prenuptial agreements. If a man gives you a hard time about it, think twice about marrying him. He may be after your money. If it's a *Rules* relationship, he won't mind a prenup. He wants nothing from you but to be with you.

By the way, there is nothing wrong with a movie star

dating or marrying her personal trainer, bodyguard, gardener, or someone who works for her and makes less money—as long as he pursued her. She should not initiate a relationship by asking him to be her date at a film screening or shower him with expensive gifts if she wants him to desire her and treat her well down the road. Invariably, men who are pursued by famous and/or wealthy women and given a life vastly better than anything they would have had on their own still manage to hurt these women or take advantage of them.

Some actresses, models, and other high-profile women convince themselves that certain men are intimidated by their beauty, fame, or wealth and that's why these men don't ask them out, and that's why they had to make the first move.

Assuming a man is intimidated by your beauty or wealth or success, why would you want to be with him? If he's too threatened to initiate a relationship with you or walk across a room to talk to you and ask for your number, then he'll be too intimidated to *be* in a relationship with you. *Rules* girls only date men who pursue them and are not intimidated by them!

If you ignore *The Rules* and make the first move toward starting a relationship with such a man, he might be flattered and go out with you, but his initial reluctance to date you will resurface down the road. Sooner or later, you'll notice him being moody or withdrawn, rather than happy to be with you. He might get angry when fans recognize you in public, resent being called by your last name, or be unhappy because you make more money than he does. He will have problems with your fame and take it out on you in some way or even leave you for someone less famous or pretty.

You may find yourself trying to change him or turn yourself inside out to make the relationship work. Ask yourself, are you willing to stop being who you are, a model, actress, or successful businesswoman to please this man? Are you interested in taking him to couples therapy to deal with his "issues" about your fame? If you're not, then date only men who are not threatened by you, who like you, and are not unduly impressed by your wealth or fame.

The truth is, some men—even very good-looking men— are sometimes simply attracted to average-looking women, not great beauties. If you're a model, you should date only men who are not intimidated by models. If you're a gorgeous movie star, you should date only men who want a gorgeous movie star. Don't try to figure it out. Think of TV shows such as *Mary Tyler Moore*—some men like Mary, some like Rhoda, or *Friends*—some men like Monica, some like Rachel.

Movie stars, socialites, and other high-profile women must do *The Rules* on the media as well as on men.

If a reporter asks you if you ever want to get married (or why such a beautiful woman such as you isn't married), don't say anything like, "Actually I thought I'd be married by now. It's the only thing missing in my life," or "I'd trade all my success for a good relationship," or "I envy my sister who's not rich or famous, but has a husband and three kids. I haven't had a good date in years."

Don't come across as depressed or cynical about love. Why reveal your personal anxieties? A press interview is not a therapy session. Don't be so open!

Instead, act confident and happy so that everyone thinks any man would be lucky to have you. Give the impression that you're not worried about your love life. Respond the same way you would to a man who asks why aren't you married. Count to five and say, "I never really thought about it" or "I'm just having fun right now!"

If you're in a relationship and reporters ask how it's going, just say "Great" and then talk about your movie, business, charity work, or whatever. Your love life is really none of their business, so be mysterious and vague, as if you were too busy to think about it. It's good for *The Rules* if you don't give away too much information.

Do not go into detail, as many famous people do, about how he's the man of your dreams, your soul mate, that you see each other all the time, or how great the sex is. Declaring your love on national television will not make him yours, scare other women away, or make him marry you. Talking openly about your relationship will only embarrass him and scare *him* away. Let *him* talk about you when he's interviewed. Better to do *The Rules* quietly and show up at the Oscars with an engagement ring than to talk for an hour about a man who hasn't proposed to you yet on a daytime talk show!

Another rule for the rich and famous: When the paparazzi snap photos of you and your boyfriend, you should not be all over him. Let him embrace *you,* pull *you* close to him, or hold *your* hand, whatever, just as long as it's all his doing. Otherwise the media and his friends will surely say, "Look who's a twosome now" and he'll get scared. And wouldn't you rather have a strong relationship that lasts a lifetime than just one more pretty picture?

## Chapter 14 ⸻

# Don't Be a Groupie and Other *Rules* for Dating Celebrities or High-Profile Men

It's not everyday that you meet a celebrity or CEO, but it can happen—at a party, on a plane, in the company cafeteria, or in a doctor's waiting room. And if you don't know *The Rules* and do them, you can easily ruin a once-in-a-lifetime opportunity.

For example, we know a woman who met a famous actor at a fund-raiser. He walked right up to her and said, "You're beautiful. When can we go out?"

Here was a perfect *Rules* beginning—he was obviously attracted to her and made the first move. But not knowing *The Rules,* she gushed, "Tonight."

Obviously, that was the wrong answer. When a famous actor says when can I see you, just smile and say, "Let me think, I don't know . . ." as if famous actors ask you out all the time. Even if he's ten times busier than you are, act as if you just don't know when you can see him. He must specifically ask you out for a particular night and it cannot be that night or the next night but several nights in advance.

The actor took our friend out to dinner, where she proceeded to tell him how much she admired his work and even asked him to autograph the menu. They spoke for hours (even closed the restaurant) and he hardly had to pressure her to go back to his hotel room. Although she did not have sex with him, she spent the night. He told her he would call her again when he was in town in a few weeks, but she never heard from him. By the time she found out about *The Rules,* it was too late.

What follows are *The Rules* for meeting and dating actors, athletes, famous authors, movie producers, directors, CEOs, and other powerful men. Assuming the celebrity or business VIP spoke to you first, here's what to do and not to do:

1. Take a deep breath. Stay composed.
2. Treat him as you would any other man—a coworker, your doorman—not the movie star or business tycoon he is.
3. Do not stare at him.
4. Do not light up or act giddy, as if you just won the lottery.
5. Do not carry on like a crazed fan. In other words, do not say anything like, "Oh my God, I can't believe it's——! I've seen all your movies!" (Even if you have seen all his movies twice!) Act as if you've been out of the country for the last three years and you're not

quite sure who he is, even if he was just on the cover of *People* magazine.

6. Don't ask for his autograph.

7. Don't compliment him, as in "You look much better in person than on TV."

8. Don't ask him about his next movie or show any interest in his career (or you'll sound like every other woman he's ever met).

9. If you're an aspiring actress, do not ask for an audition or a part in his movie. If you're looking for work, do not ask this high-powered executive for a job in his company. Do not ask for his business card or offer to send him your résumé or movie script.

10. Do not ask him to do you a favor, such as donate money to your favorite charity or give you tickets to his show or a free copy of his book.

11. Act interested, but not spellbound. Movie stars and CEOs are typically hounded and drooled over. So leave him alone. After five or ten minutes of conversation about whatever he wants to talk about, say, "Oh, look at the time. I must leave now. It was nice meeting you" and walk away. Do not spend the evening talking to this man. Do not agree to go out with him that night, even if he's leaving the country the next morning. (He can always call you—they have phones in other countries, too.)

12. Do not seem impressed by his Armani suit, limo, or entourage.

13. If you meet a performer and he offers you a ticket to see his concert or show as a first date, politely de-

cline. Attending his show is not a date. If he wants to see you the night of the show, he must pick you up afterward and take you out.

14. If you're dating a sports star, don't run around the country wearing his jersey and attending all his games until you're in a committed relationship. Even then, he still must ask you out on dates to spend time with you.

15. Once you're actually dating a CEO or celebrity, don't see him whenever and wherever it's convenient for him because *he* has a busy schedule. He still has to ask you out in advance and you must turn him down politely if he expects to see you only on his terms—otherwise he will take you for granted. Celebrities are used to being spoiled, but you're a *Rules* girl!

16. Of course, it's tempting to drop your friends and family and revolve your whole life around this famous man. By following *The Rules,* you must still live your own life, see him only two to three times a week—until he proposes.

17. If he's handsome or widely popular, expect that other women might write him, call him, and throw themselves at him in public. Do not get angry or show jealousy or insecurity when this happens. Do not be possessive in public. If he pursued you and you're doing *The Rules,* their advances won't matter. He'll still want you!

18. Be discreet. Do not call the tabloids and tell them you're dating a celebrity, as a way of announcing to other women or the world that he's yours—that

doesn't work anyway—and don't talk to reporters if they call you. That would be self-serving, possibly hurtful or embarrassing to him, and might ruin any chances of his continuing to see you.

19. Don't try to become friendly with his secretary, publicist, or limo driver in an effort to keep tabs on him or so they put in a good word for you.

20. Don't seem overly interested in his fame, his wealth or the limelight. *Rules* girls are not groupies!

Keep in mind, sometimes a star is *not* your Mr. Right, and sometimes your Mr. Right is not a star. If you truly want things to work out between you, take things slowly, get to know him, and determine whether you love *him* or his image.

# Observe His Behavior on the Holidays

How he treats you on the holidays is a good barometer of how he feels about you!

When a man is in love, he thinks about you and makes special plans with you *in advance* of Valentine's Day, New Year's Eve, your birthday, and Christmas or its equivalent. He'll circle the dates on his calendar and try to get the best table at a romantic restaurant—and that could mean calling a week or two ahead of time!

If it's Valentine's Day, he'll call the florist to buy you roses or your favorite flowers. If it's your birthday, he might buy you a piece of jewelry and a meaningful card. He might suggest you spend the holidays with his family, and make sure you ring in the New Year together in a romantic way. He'll make a thoughtful toast about the two of you. You're always on his mind and in his heart.

He looks forward to being with you on that special night and watching you read his card and open his present.

What should you give him? A *Rules* girl gives a man she is dating *a simple card* for Valentine's Day—something short and sweet; no poetry and no balloons—and maybe a scarf or sweater for his birthday or the holidays. (See Chapter 16: "Don't Go Overboard and Other *Rules* for Giving to Men.")

When a man is not in love, he sometimes doesn't even acknowledge the holidays. He may take you out on Saturday night as he usually does and not even mention the holiday—even if it falls the next day—hoping that you don't either. You may blame his lack of romantic interest in you at holiday time on his upbringing or past relationships, but a man in love with a woman acts differently with her than with anyone else.

If he's really not planning to marry you, he may not even call you the week of Valentine's Day or New Year's Eve. He may just skip the week to avoid the whole issue. If you ask him why he didn't call, he might say things were hectic at work or holidays are silly. But a man in love would not be too busy or cynical about the holidays. In fact, we've known a few men who even carved pumpkins for their girlfriends on Halloween, hardly an important occasion.

When a man is not in love, he may buy a silly card and just sign his name—with no "love." He finds the holidays stupid or commercial and gets irritable if you take it seriously or expect more from him.

If the man you are dating does little or nothing for your birthday, Valentine's Day, or New Year's Eve, what should you do?

Don't bring up the occasion either. Pretend you forgot or didn't care—and then cry to your girlfriends. Just don't let him know it bothered you!

Don't have a "talk" about how you thought your first Valentine's Day or birthday together would be more romantic and are really disappointed and hurt. You can't make a man feel romantic if he doesn't. If these special occasions are not important to him you must accept this.

Don't hint that it's Valentine's Day, or pressure him to take you out or buy you flowers. He either thought of it and wanted to or he didn't. Don't try to get something from the wrong source. Buy yourself flowers, if that's important to you.

If you demand that he take you out or buy you flowers, he may comply, but it won't be from his heart. He may do it just to avoid an argument or to continue to see you (until he meets someone else) or to have sex. It never works *long-term* if we force things.

If the man you are dating did not ask you out on New Year's Eve or Valentine's Day or did not suggest spending Christmas together, you cannot ask him to. Man must pursue woman! Do not offer to make him a candlelit dinner at your place (to make it easy for him or so that he doesn't have to plan or spend money). If he didn't initiate a romantic evening with you, then he didn't want to be romantic with you. Just put it in the back of your head that this man is not romantic or not in love with you and either accept that or move on. This is a good time to reevaluate the relationship and to determine if he is your Mr. Right.

On Valentine's Days and New Year's Eves in the past—before you discovered *The Rules*—you may have overlooked signs that a man wasn't in love with you. You may have rationalized his no card/silly card, and told yourself these gestures were not important. But in your heart, you knew the truth. You knew that a man in love would have bought you flowers or tried to do something special.

Now that you know *The Rules,* what do you do that night if the man you are dating did not ask you out at least several days—preferably a week—in advance for an important occasion?

Make plans with friends or go to a party where you might meet someone else. The holidays can be a very lonely and painful time for a single woman, so try not to be home by yourself.

But even if all you do is stay home, make sure to leave your answering machine on so, in case he calls, he doesn't know where you are. It really doesn't matter what you do that night as long as you don't—in a weak moment—call him and invite him over. Rent a video or invite a girlfriend over for dinner, and think seriously about breaking up with this guy. Resolve to do *The Rules* on every man you meet from this moment on so you don't spend your next birthday/Valentine's Day/New Year's Eve/Christmas, or holiday alone!

# Don't Go Overboard and Other *Rules* for Giving to Men

As we explained in *The Rules,* you should not offer to pay for anything on the first three dates. There's no need to. When a man is interested in you, he is not thinking about money (i.e., splitting the check), he's hoping to make a good impression and hoping that you'll see him again. Part of pursuing you is making plans and paying for everything.

Of course, if he *asks* you to split the check, cheerfully do so. You weren't trying to get a free meal. You want him to *want* to pay for you. We don't tell a man to pick up the check. We just notice he didn't and put it in the back of our mind. Maybe he's not Mr. Right.

We are not telling you to be a gold digger. It is not about how much he spends. Let him take you to an inexpensive restaurant or a movie, as long as he plans ahead and pays for the date. When a man is truly in love, he'll work extra hours or borrow from his parents or friends to come up with the money to impress you. Dutch treat is fine for friends and coworkers, not dates. You want a man who is crazy about you!

Women, especially those making good salaries, tend to get hung up on reciprocating. We tell them that in the first two to three months of dating they should be focusing instead on getting off the phone first and not asking a man out—not obsessing about buying him dinner or a tie. When you're married, you can buy him anything you want!

After three months, you can make or buy him dinner.

On his birthday and/or other gift-giving holidays, *The Rules* are:

Do not spend more than $50 to $100, even if you can well afford to. But more importantly, don't buy him anything romantic.

*Good gift ideas include:*

1. A book on a subject of interest to him, as long as it has nothing to do with astrology, therapy, love or relationships, such as business, politics, computers, or a novel (nonromantic) you know he'd love to read.
2. A winter scarf.
3. A T-shirt, sweatshirt, or cap of his favorite sports team.

*Do not buy him:*

1. Jewelry.
2. Anything monogrammed.

3. A picture frame or photo album.
4. Champagne glasses, or any houseware for that matter.
5. A book of poems.

Women are not only too generous to men in material ways—they tend to be too extending in social situations as well. They invite a man they just started dating to accompany them to a wedding, dinner party, business or family function, country club, summer house, or business trip/vacation. We strongly suggest you do not do so for at least three months. If you do, he will surely feel that you are more serious about the relationship than he is, get scared and pull back. In addition, if he is surrounded by married couples at these events, he will most surely feel pressured.

If you are in a business where you get free tickets to tennis matches, trips, or are regularly invited to business parties and shows as part of your job, do not take him for the first few months. Take a friend or go alone. Why?

1. You will not be mysterious if he knows your entire social calendar.
2. He should not think of you as a cash cow. Otherwise, how will you know if he really cares about *you* or your perks? He must fall in love with you *first!*
3. When a man is in love with you, he wants to be with *you*. If you are always giving him presents and taking him to places, he might believe you are trying to buy his love and affection, that you are trying too hard, and care too much, which is never good.

One more way a woman may try to give too much to a man is by being overly involved in his life. Needless to say, you can listen and offer suggestions, but don't become wrapped up in his business problems, family affairs, or any other issues. You are not his therapist or his wife (yet).

Actually, the best gift you can give a man is to do *The Rules,* which gives him the thrill of pursuing you and the glory of getting you!

# Chapter 17 _____

# Buyer Beware (Weeding out Mr. Wrong)!

*The Rules* are not about marrying the first man you are attracted to who calls you by Wednesday for Saturday night and buys you flowers. It's about marrying your own personal Mr. Right—a man whom you love and whose character you admire and can live with.

Love may be blind, but *Rules* girls are not stupid! In addition to doing *The Rules,* you should be observing his behavior in various situations to decide if he's right for you. You may want to keep notes in *The Rules Dating Journal* to keep track of what he says and how he acts in his relationship with you. For example, is he a man of his word or does he promise and not deliver? Does he speak badly about people or tell horrible stories about ex-girlfriends? Is he cheap on dates? Is he critical of you? Does he drink or smoke too much? Is he rude to waiters? If either of you has been married before, how does he treat his children or your children?

It's easy to ignore certain behavior, but if it's written down in black and white, you will see a pattern emerge and not be able to lie to yourself or sweep it under the rug.

Don't marry thinking you will change this kind of behavior—people don't usually change that much. We believe that anything you don't like about the man you marry was there when you were dating him—you just didn't really think about it seriously or told yourself you didn't mind.

A woman we know who followed *The Rules* called us one day to say Mr. Right had proposed. We were thrilled, but we quickly got suspicious when she told us that six months had passed and he still hadn't committed to a wedding date. She, too, felt something was wrong, but she really wanted to marry this man. We advised her to try to pin him down to a date. When she did, he admitted that he was back with his ex-girlfriend.

If something doesn't feel right to you about a man, it probably isn't! If you don't want to be miserable and full of regrets later on, you have to pay attention now. *Rules* girls don't sleep at the wheel!

No, *Rules* girls take a very active role in choosing Mr. Right. At first glance, *The Rules* may seem like passive dating—let him call you, let him ask you out, let him pick you up, let him do all the work. In terms of the *chase*, that's certainly true. But we are also telling women to actively evaluate a man's character and behavior. Did he call when he said he'd call? Did he remember your birthday?

\* \* \*

A *Rules* girl is always carefully observing his behavior and taking notes. This *is* active, not passive, dating.

When we told you to "be quiet and mysterious, act lady-like, and cross your legs and smile and don't talk so much" on the first few dates, we did not mean that you shouldn't *think!* We told you this for two reasons:

(a) so you don't tell him your whole life story too soon and live to regret it, and, equally important,

(b) so you *listen.* The less you talk, the more you can hear and pick up clues if he's right for you.

Sometimes a woman is so anxious to get married to a man she is attracted to—a man who is chasing her thanks to *The Rules*—that she blocks out traits she doesn't like about him. She hopes that love and marriage will change him in time. We say, maybe, maybe not. It's true that former playboy types lose interest in the club scene when they meet a *Rules* girl and become fond of changing diapers when they have a child. But we also say, what you see is what you get, so don't count on a man changing.

Let's look at some specific dilemmas you might be facing:

**Dilemma #1:** You're amazed—and impressed—by his sophistication with alcohol. He puts away countless gin and tonics without a problem, and you're charmed by the way he orders the best bottle of wine at romantic restaurants! But after reading this chapter, you remember that most of the time you had mineral water and *he* gladly drank the whole bottle.

*Buyer beware:* Love won't change an addiction and

heavy drinking isn't charming when you have kids to support and he's throwing money away at bars, or you are the designated driver after every party. If you think he drinks too much, don't marry him unless he agrees to seek help and has stopped drinking for at least a year. It's good for him and it's good for you.

**Dilemma #2:** You think you've found Mr. Right, except that he'd rather read the newspaper or work on the computer than have sex with you most week nights and even Sunday mornings. Now that you're reading this chapter, you remember that he was always a little too intellectual for your taste. You wished he were more passionate, not so cerebral.

*Buyer beware:* This will be a problem in your marriage if sex and passion are important to you.

**Dilemma #3:** He's very good-looking, personable, and a ton of fun, but not as deep as you would like him to be. You are a serious reader—you tend to be analytical and you are into yoga and meditation. He likes action sports, such as tennis and basketball. You want to have soulful discussions; he's more pragmatic.

*Buyer beware:* This will be a problem if you like to have philosophical conversations with your mate. Just know that he may ask you to have breakfast with him or play tennis when you're in the middle of yoga or meditating.

**Dilemma #4:** He's into a whirlwind courtship. He calls you day and night and proposes after a month or two. You think he's a little impulsive, but you're also thrilled!

*Buyer beware:* If you allow yourself to get caught up in a whirlwind romance and move at his speed, you may live to regret it. You need to pace the relationship—to wait and allow yourself time to observe his behavior in many different situations—before you make such a serious commitment. Otherwise, you may find out *after* you're married that he's a womanizer, gambler, emotionally immature, in deep financial debt, or has a criminal past. By then it might be too late.

**Dilemma #5:** He's exciting and debonair, but he has a dark side. You've heard him scream at his family, his friends, and even business associates.

*Buyer beware:* He may yell or be violent toward you or your children.

**Dilemma #6:** He loves you, but is often a drop annoyed by your close girlfriends, your family, and any man who pays too much attention to you. He gets angry if you don't tell him everything or include him in everything.

*Buyer beware:* While it's flattering to be the center of a man's attention, as opposed to being ignored, know that you might have fights about his level of involvement in your day-to-day activities.

Sometimes the problem is not his character, but circumstances, such as:

**Dilemma #7:** You love him, but he's much older than you, divorced, and a devoted father to two teenagers. You never cared for children, much less stepchildren.

*Buyer beware:* You may resent his children and the time they take away from your relationship. You might also resent the amount of money he is paying to his ex-wife to support them.

Sometimes the problem is not him at all, but *you*. Your motives are not so good, such as:

**Dilemma #8:** You love him but, truth be told, you wouldn't be marrying him if he wasn't also rich.

*Buyer beware:* What are you going to do if his business sours and he no longer can buy you diamonds and fur coats? What if you actually have to go back to work?

In the above scenarios, we are not saying "don't marry him." We are simply saying go into the marriage with your eyes open. Be honest with yourself! Check your motives! *Rules* girls don't get married at any cost!

If you don't want to have problems later on, think twice about marrying for money or power, unless you can live with the downside. Think twice about marrying to get even with your ex-husband who left you for a younger woman or to escape a bad home life. Think twice about marrying anyone simply to have children.

And don't be lax about discussing major issues such as religion or whether to have children *before* you get married.

\*　　\*　　\*

While making sure you are marrying Mr. Right is not always so easy, by doing *The Rules* you at least weed out Mr. Wrong.

For example, any man who is interested in you just for sex, money, or convenience automatically loses interest because you are not sleeping with him right away, you are not supporting him, and you are not meeting him when and where it's convenient for him.

A man has to *really care about you* to call you early in the week (every week), make plans, pick you up, and wait until you're ready to have sex! Mr. Wrongs simply won't put up with the rigors of *The Rules*—they move on to women without such standards.

So while you're doing *The Rules,* you should also be observing, writing, and thinking, *Is he the right one for me?* Take an active role—your long-term happiness is definitely worth the work.

*Chapter 18* _____

# Closing the Deal (Getting Him to the Altar)

We're not talking about a business deal here, but getting the man you want to propose and then to turn that proposal into an actual wedding date—a feat some women would say can be tougher than any corporate transaction. Of course, it's made much easier by doing *The Rules*.

If you've been following *The Rules* from the moment you met Mr. Right and he says he loves you, he *will* propose—sometimes in a matter of a few months, but usually within fifteen months. (He may have his own "rules" about dating you for four seasons before proposing, and there's nothing wrong with that.)

By doing *The Rules* you will not only get a proposal, but you will know where the relationship is going long before he pops the question. You will sense a warm, open feeling emanating from him, a desire to include you in his world. Here are some of the key words and phrases he is likely to bring up in conversations with you:

1. The future—whether it be where he wants to live, his career goals, or the car he is planning to buy.
2. Marriage (the M-word)—for example, he'll *volunteer* that he's going to be the best man when his friend gets married.
3. Kids—he might mention his nephew's upcoming birthday.
4. Married friends—he might discuss his married friends or suggest doubling with them.
5. His family—he'll talk about his parents and ask you about yours or invite you to a family gathering for the holidays.

He'll also include you in the most minute details of his day—i.e., he'll tell you that he got a haircut or he washed the car. He's always bringing you closer to him.

Because you let him pursue you, didn't see him more than two or three times a week, refused to go away with him on week-long vacations, have not moved in or crowded him in any way, you've actually helped him to fall in love with you and *want* to marry you. He wants more of you, not less.

Within a year, if not sooner, he's figured out that he not only *wants* to marry you but *has* to marry you to see you more often, to really have you.

Your problem is not *if* he's going to marry you, but *when. Men can date for five years!* They are notorious for wanting to put off the actual engagement part until *later*. If he suggests living together first to see if you get along or to see you more often, tell him you're old-fashioned and want to wait until you're engaged or married.

A man can love you, but marriage . . . that's a little scary. Maybe he's just trying to hold on to his bachelorhood, maybe he's been married before and isn't in any rush to do it again, or maybe he's young (under twenty-five years old).

In general, the way to get a man to ask you to marry him in a reasonable amount of time is not to live with him before you're engaged or married and to continue to see him only three times a week, even though by this time you *want* to be inseparable.

If that doesn't work, you might have to shake things up a little bit—go away for a weekend with a girlfriend, cancel a Saturday night date, get very busy at work, mention that you are renewing your apartment lease, and be mysterious about your activities. All of the above should make him anxious to propose. As you already know, a man who is wary of commitment is made less wary by a woman moving *away* from, not *toward,* commitment. This isn't trickery. You're just giving him *space.*

On the other hand, if you have not done *The Rules* all along, getting a man to propose can be very difficult.

If you have been dating a man for two, three, or even five years and he has not proposed, you might be thinking that if you hang around long enough, he will eventually ask. You have probably accepted his excuses—financial problems, married before, not ready, and so on—as to why he can't marry you just yet. But now that you've read *The Rules,* you know that a *Rules* girl doesn't date a man forever and the way to get him to propose (if he's going to propose at all) is *not* to hang around.

Let's say you've been dating him for more than a year and he's somehow avoided the whole issue of marriage and the future, what should you do?

Ask him his intentions. If he says he has no plans to marry you, say "Okay" and then never see him again. Men don't lie about things like this. He's not scared of commitment—he doesn't want to marry you.

If he says he does plan to marry you some day, then it's up to you to *close the deal.* Ask him when and if it's more than a year, see less of him and think about dating others. You've already spent more than a year waiting for him to propose, do you have another year to wait?

If you are already living together (because you found out about *The Rules* after you moved in) and he says he doesn't want to get engaged, make plans to move out. But don't say, "I'm moving out because you won't commit." That would be too obvious. Just say you need more space and that you heard about a great apartment or your friend is renting hers. When a man doesn't want to commit, we leave him alone. If he doesn't try to stop you or get you back with a proposal, don't waste your time. If he asks what's going on, nonchalantly answer, "I don't know if this relationship is for me." If he can live without you, you don't want him. You move on.

Here are five things *not* to do, no matter how tempting:

1. Don't tell him you're hurt, mad, or reprimand him for wasting your time or leading you on. You lived with him—no one twisted your arm. Take responsibility for your actions. By not doing *The Rules,* you allowed him to be with you indefinitely. In a *Rules* relationship a man either proposes within a year—two years at the max!—or it's next!

2. Don't suggest going to couples therapy to discuss why *he* can't commit. Men can and do commit when they love you and you do *The Rules* on them. But they can become "commitment-phobic" when a woman has pursued them, is too available, or they're just not in love with her. They say things like, "I find marriage a difficult concept to swallow," or they conveniently cite the high divorce rate.

3. Don't let a man brainwash you into thinking that marriage isn't important—"just a piece of paper"—and that as long as you're together that's all that matters. If he doesn't want to marry you then he's not *that* in love with you, or it's not the brand of love you want. What it really means is he still wants the option of meeting someone else!

4. Don't let a man convince you that because he's been married before he can't marry you or that you should give him time to recover from Wife No. 1 or 2.

5. Don't let a man you have been dating for years convince you to wait until "things slow down" at work or he's better off financially to make a commitment. This is the worst reason. There will always be work/money issues in life. They should have nothing to do with

marrying you. When a man loves you and wants to marry you he hopes you *don't* notice these issues, or he includes you in their solutions and begs you to marry him anyway. He gets down on one bended knee and says something like, "Look, I know I'm not a millionaire, but I love you and I'd do anything for you." When a man says "You're too good for me," what he really means is "I don't want you."

In conclusion, the same man who won't commit because of issues with his ex-wife or his finances has no problem proposing to a woman who refused to date him longer than a year. Sometimes a man will date a woman for five years claiming he has commitment issues and after breaking up with her, easily marries someone else in six months.

If you are involved with a man for several years who isn't proposing, how much longer are you willing to wait? When a man knows that you will accept less than marriage he is not motivated to fully commit himself. You must be willing to walk away from a dead-end relationship.

Assuming you are engaged, how do you get him to walk down the aisle?

The truth is, if you're engaged as a result of *The Rules*, getting him to marry you should not be a problem. There's no "cold feet" in *Rules* engagements. In fact, just the opposite is the case. He's made his decision, he *wants* to get married, to be with you all the time, forever.

There's usually a wondrous, exciting planning of the

wedding. He's calling caterers, videographers, and tuxedo places, and driving himself crazy trying to pick the most meaningful wedding song. He's intimately involved in every detail of the wedding. He's worried that you might not get your dress in time. The *only* time he is angry at you is when you're not making the wedding your top priority.

Of course, getting engaged is no *guarantee* of marriage, so don't get lax about *The Rules* when you're engaged. Don't think you can talk to him on the phone for hours, and it's still best not to move in together yet. Engagements can be broken and wedding dates postponed or never set. If you move in, he may change his mind and decide not to marry you so soon! Better that he miss you and move up the wedding date than feel claustrophobic as you take over his closet space.

Also, be on the alert for any special circumstances or excuses your fiancé might make, such as:

1. He thinks being engaged is great, but why rush marriage?
2. He's been married before, it was a disaster, and he's not anxious to tie the knot again. He gave you the ring so he doesn't lose you (so you won't sleep with anyone else), but he's happy with the status quo.
3. He's young and still likes to go out with his friends, not be tied down. He likes the bachelor life and although you convinced him to get engaged, you can't pin him down for a wedding date. You have a ring, but you're not sure what the future looks like.

4. You were already living together when you got engaged, but you still don't have a wedding date set. What to do?

In general, we feel that when you get engaged you should set a wedding date. *Rules* engagements are usually a year or less. If you're young (under twenty-five), a two-year engagement is fine.

If the engagement is dragging on, you may want to think about giving him back the ring and moving on. Perhaps he's not Mr. Right. *Rules* girls don't waste time.

## Not Closing the Deal (Being True to Yourself)

Perhaps you're the one having second thoughts. You did *The Rules,* he may or may not have proposed, but now you're having doubts about him and the relationship. Something just doesn't feel right, you're thinking about breaking it off. Perhaps you're finding out that he's not the man of your dreams after all, or there are just extenuating circumstances. What should you do?

If you've thought about it carefully and discussed your decision with a therapist, good friends, or family members, we suggest you *always* trust your instincts. *Do Not Close the Deal.*

Don't feel silly, embarrassed, or guilty. Don't hate yourself or feel like a failure or that you wasted a year or two of your life. You didn't. Ending a relationship that isn't right is a learning and growing experience. Besides, you're not the first woman to change her mind or cancel a wedding. It happens sometimes. You tried, it didn't work out, much better to find out and disentangle yourself now than later on. Don't stay with him because you're a couple, you've made future plans together, you like his parents, you're entrenched and it feels complicated to break it off at this stage of the game.

After you've made up your mind, give yourself time and permission to cry and grieve. Who wouldn't be upset? It's normal. But don't give up on love or throw yourself in front of a bus. Keep the faith. Always remember, there's another person out there—the real Mr. Right—for you and you're a winner for being honest with yourself! Pump yourself up by rereading *The Rules,* specifically **Rule #1:** *You are a Creature Unlike Any Other:* You trust in the abundance and goodness of the universe: if not him, someone better . . . Any man would be lucky to have you! Plan a social action, get back on track! Keep doing *The Rules.* Your *real* Mr. Right may be just around the corner and when you meet him, you won't regret past breakups!

# Don't Be the Rebound Girl and Other *Rules* for Dating a Man Who Is Separated

If you have been following *The Rules,* you are not dating a married man for all the obvious reasons. It's not honest, he's not yours, and you could waste a lot of time waiting for him to leave his wife, if he ever does.

Many women have called us to say they are dating a married man anyway. To these women, all we can suggest is that they find the courage—pray for it, do whatever it takes—to stop seeing him. Dating a married man is like driving down a dead-end street—it gets you nowhere. Better to date him when he's divorced and available. So don't call him, don't write him letters, don't initiate encounters, and don't meet him at a moment's notice.

Be sure the man you are dating is at the very least separated from his wife. But don't assume he is. How can you tell? If he doesn't give you his home number, tells you the best way to get in touch with him is by his beeper or gives you a phone number but he's never there when you call, doesn't introduce you to family or friends, and acts on the secretive side, then you must wonder! Something is off. Be on the alert. He might be trying to juggle two lives. You'll find out soon enough if you do *The Rules* and pay attention.

So now, hopefully, you are dating a man who is *really* separated. That can be messy enough! There's his ex-wife, money issues, lawyers, and sometimes complicated custody battles. It might feel like walking into the middle of a movie. Are you willing to deal with all these issues and a possibly lengthy courtship?

If you are, here are some rules:

In addition to following all the rules for dating a single man, you must *pay attention* to what he says about why his marriage didn't work out and how it might affect his chances of marrying and *staying* married to you. If he doesn't talk about the breakup, try to find out (without being too obvious) whether it was his idea or hers to get a divorce.

This information is important. If the divorce was his idea, it probably means he isn't hung up on his ex—a good sign. On the other hand, it also shows that he is capable of leaving a woman and that he could walk out on you one day. If you have been able to surmise that it wasn't a *Rules* marriage—in other words, she pursued him—and your relationship is, you have nothing to worry about. He just wanted out of a bad marriage.

But if you think he just picked up and left one day for no good reason, keep your eye on him. He could be bad news. Fortunately, *The Rules* will help you screen out any disturbing behavior and inconsistencies—skipping a Saturday night date here and there, a few no-shows, forgetting your birthday—long before you walk down the aisle.

If it was his wife's idea to end the marriage, realize that he may still have feelings for her and there's a chance they could get back together. This is particularly true if he is newly separated—say, under six months. He may be dating you merely as a *distraction*—as a way of helping himself get over his ex. If he talks about *her* all the time when he's with you, then he's not crazy in love with you! Remember, you want to be his *Rules* girl, not his rebound girl!

So be on the lookout for signs that he finds excuses to contact her, still fights with her a lot and gets very emotional about the separation. That's not how he should behave when he's over her and in love with you! When a man is not interested in staying with an ex, he has little to do with her and does not try to prolong the divorce for any reason. He just wants it over.

Whatever the case is, don't play therapist to his marital problems. If he always wants to talk about the breakup, listen politely for a little while here and there, but don't give him advice and don't help him put down his ex-wife if he has a habit of doing so. He can put down his ex-wife, but you shouldn't. Don't show jealousy or seem too interested if he is in contact with her. The less you appear to care, the better.

Don't resolve to be the "nicer second wife" if and when he marries you. For example, if he complains that his ex-wife was too busy with her career and not there enough for him, you might think you shouldn't do *The Rules,* that you can't end dates first because he's so needy and you should put him before your career. You might decide to see him constantly, cook meals on the weekends for him to have during the week—literally, *take care of him.* This is a big mistake. We know women who played therapist/nurse, became the *woman who understands,* spent years on a man, only to see him remarry someone just like his ex! Whatever he may say about his ex-wife, remember, *he married her.* On some level, he likes that type. You can't always go by what a man says—it's what he does that counts. Just do *The Rules* and be true to yourself.

Remember, when you are dating a man who is separated, it is easy to get caught up in his problems, his schedule, his timetable, his needs. For example, he might say that he doesn't want to remarry "for a while" until things settle down or that he wants to wait until his children can handle all the changes, not to mention a stepmom.

Be understanding, but not *too* understanding. *Rules* girls don't wait forever. If he is serious about marrying you, there is no reason why he shouldn't be divorced within a year after meeting you or as soon as possible. You should be engaged within six months after his divorce comes through. You should have a wedding date *set* soon after you are engaged.

Keep in mind that these are general guidelines—don't be difficult or inflexible if there are children involved or extenuating circumstances. You should only be concerned if he avoids the whole subject of marriage or wants you to live with him first. In either case, you might have to reevaluate or stop seeing him for a while. *Rules* girls don't wait indefinitely for men to sort out their lives. Don't spoil him by waiting. If he needs more than two years to remarry, he may not be *your* Mr. Right.

The fact that he has children should not change this time structure too much, but it does mean that you need to be especially considerate of his relationship with his kids. Sometimes you really must take a backseat, sometimes you have to exhibit the patience of a saint.

Don't ask to meet his children. He must include you in that part of his life when he's ready and wants to. You never want to be in a situation where his kids resent you or blame you for his marital problems or feel that you are taking their father away from them. *He* should deal with their anger. He should explain to them that he loves you and that his marriage failed on its own, that it had nothing to do with you. You shouldn't get involved.

Don't be jealous if at times he puts his children before you—i.e., he can't have Sunday brunch with you because he must see his son play soccer. His desire to be a good father, his loyalty to his children are qualities to be proud of and admire—not to be resentful of. Bite your tongue, stay busy. Don't make him feel that he has to choose between you and his children. If you plan to be their stepmom one day, then you must also think of their needs, in addition to your own.

Although we are asking you to be considerate about his relationship with his kids—and divorce can be traumatic for any child—we are not telling you to be a doormat. We know men who ask their girlfriends to be baby-sitters, or take their daughter ice-skating, but they never propose. You are not a baby-sitter or the girlfriend who is there for him, who waits and waits forever.

Dating a man who is separated can be difficult. But by doing *The Rules*, you don't put your life on hold indefinitely. You don't make excuses to yourself about why he won't remarry or why he needs years to heal from his divorce. When you do *The Rules*, a man who is separated recovers pretty quickly and happily marries you!

## Chapter 20

# A *Rules* Refresher for Married Women

If you're married, do you need to do *The Rules*? Married women who recently discovered *The Rules* often ask us this question. Although we touched upon this issue in **Rule #26** ("Even if You're Engaged or Married, You Still Need *The Rules*") in our first book, there has been a demand for more advice. In this chapter, we delve into the subject more deeply and offer tips for both *Rules* and non-*Rules* relationships.

If you did *The Rules* when you were dating your husband, you don't have to consciously play hard to get anymore. Your husband is *naturally* crazy about you. Because you did not see him all the time or talk to him for hours on the phone, he does not take you for granted and he is not bored with you. He still finds you interesting and exciting, even years later. He sees you as the prom queen and considers himself lucky to have won your affections . . . and that feeling never goes away. You have a wonderful sense of security.

*Rules* husbands are very involved. They're always calling, they initiate romance, and buy flowers or romantic gifts for your birthday, anniversary, and Valentine's Day. (And they remember all three without your help!)

*Rules* husbands like to do just about everything as a couple or a family. They take marriage very seriously. They don't complain about marriage or make jokes about you—calling you "the old ball and chain"—the way some of their unhappy friends do. Because you did *The Rules*, the way things are in the beginning can last forever—all the more reason to do *The Rules* strictly from the moment Mr. Right comes into your life.

In a *Rules* marriage, any work you have to do is on yourself—being happy or easy to be with, pursuing your career and interests, staying fit—not figuring out how to get your husband's attention.

What if you are in a non-*Rules* marriage and would like to improve your relationship? There are two kinds of non-*Rules* marriages: (1) he pursued you but you broke rules (i.e., saw him all the time, stayed on the phone for hours, or were too needy), and (2) you pursued him (called him, asked him out, initiated trips and so on).

The first situation is simple to remedy. Since he pursued you, if you start doing *The Rules* now, he'll be drawn to you all over again. Some suggestions: Don't ask him constantly if he loves you, don't remind him incessantly that it's Valentine's Day or demand flowers, don't suggest having talks, don't call him at work so often, get off the phone first when he calls, dress sexier, get involved in your own life, and work on being less needy and more independent.

Don't worry that it might feel strange to suddenly behave differently with him after a number of years. Just do *The Rules*. Men don't necessarily care or question *why* a woman is busy taking care of herself and is more positive, they just appreciate the difference and want her more.

But if *you* initiated the relationship with your husband and now find yourself unhappy because you wish he paid more attention to you, it may not be so easy. Start doing *The Rules*, first and foremost, for yourself and your self-esteem.

If you initiated sex, romance, weekend plans, or vacations when you were dating your husband and continue to in your marriage, then just stop being the pursuer, the planner, and the one who makes all romantic overtures. Do this for a week, two weeks, or even a month, and see what happens.

By doing *The Rules*—leaving your husband alone—he'll appreciate the space and you'll be clearer about how he really feels about you. He may miss your attention and start pursuing you, or not miss it at all. By doing *The Rules*, you'll find out. You'll let nature take its course.

Below are sixteen suggestions which, in addition to **Rule #26,** will improve your marriage:

1. *Start with your looks.*

    If your husband is not paying attention to you, is it in any way warranted? Take a good look at yourself! Have you gained a lot of weight? (Is the tread-mill in your bedroom being used just to hang clothes?) When was the last time you had a manicure or new hairstyle? Do you need some new stylish/sexy clothes?

Instead of demanding that your husband pay more attention to you or wishing his pretty secretary (who's only thin because *she's* never had kids) would quit or get fired, start on a self-improvement plan today. Don't tell yourself all this is superficial or that you have more important things to do. Appearance counts and there's no reason why your husband shouldn't find you hot and sexy. Pretend you're dating him all over again!

Starting this minute, go on a diet if you need to, exercise, grow your hair longer, get a makeover, and treat yourself to a manicure and pedicure. Looks aren't everything, but try not to scrimp on them or on your clothes. It never hurts to look the best you can. You will feel good and he will like it!

2. *Use your mind.*

Some women complain that their husbands aren't interested in them when the truth is they're doing little or nothing to make their own lives meaningful. Just as we told single women to "Fill up before the date" in *The Rules,* we encourage married women to get involved in *something* outside of their relationship with their husbands. It could be their work, their friends, volunteer work for a charity, furthering their education, taking up a hobby or sport, or simply reading the newspaper or a book.

3. *Don't analyze and reanalyze your relationship or force him to talk about it.*

It's no secret that women like to talk about their feelings and the "relationship" more than men do. If you feel the need to have a heart-to-heart talk with your husband, but suspect that he's not interested at that very moment, a good *Rules* credo is to wait. Talk to a friend instead. It's rarely a good conversation when he's not in the mood. Don't analyze why he doesn't want to talk. If you are relaxed and confident about your relationship, he'll be much more likely to want to discuss it with you.

Besides, unless a talk is absolutely necessary, sometimes the best way to get your husband's attention is to look extra good and be pleasant and enthusiastic with him about your life as it currently is.

4. *Leave him alone.*

If your husband wants to watch a football game or sit in his La-Z-Boy chair with the newspaper, try not to disturb him. Men like to go inward at times—and these are the worst times to try to get him to do something together. Accept that he's in his own world and get busy in yours!

If you interrupt him, he will feel annoyed and you might feel rejected and unloved. It's better to get involved in something of your own; he will seek you out when he's done with whatever he was doing. A marriage works better when husband pursues wife!

5. *Don't be a nag.*

Don't constantly complain about the lack of money, the size of your house, what needs to be done in the house, or tell him what your friends have and what you don't have. Hopefully, you married for love, not other reasons. Remember that, and don't let your relationship become adversarial. Instead of trying to make your husband feel inadequate, focus on the positive. Tell him how happy you are with him, your life, and your marriage.

Married women often complain that their husbands don't help around the house enough or don't really listen. Sometimes their gripes are valid, but nagging isn't the answer. If you constantly harp on his faults, he will simply learn to tune you out.

All you can do is ask him—once and nicely!—to make an effort to do this or that. But accept that he may or may not change. Remember, don't expect him to change to make you happy—work on accepting him as he is and focus on making yourself the best you can be.

6. *Let him initiate romance.*

Some married women wish their husbands came home with flowers more often. If your husband doesn't always act like a Hallmark relationship card, don't be angry and resentful. He married you! Don't expect him to prove his love to you everyday. Are you always romantic and loving when he comes home?

In *The Rules,* we told single women not to initiate romance because man must pursue woman and because you can easily get hurt if your advances are rejected. Now that you're married, of course you can initiate romance or sex, but only if you accept that he may or may not be in the mood. He could be preoccupied with problems at work. Can you take what appears to be rejection if he's not in the mood at the moment? Know your own limitations, and act accordingly.

7. *Don't be jealous.*

Instead of worrying about every woman he talks to at a party, put your energy into being confident and having fun at the party yourself. Don't cling to his side, but walk around and mingle. Jealousy is a chink in your armor. Your husband should not think that you'd be lost without him. *Rules* women actually think the opposite. They tell themselves, "Any man would be lucky to have me!"

Jealousy doesn't work anyway. *Rules* women don't waste time on behaviors that don't work. They're busy with their careers, kids, friends, hobbies, and learning new skills. So don't waste your time watching his every move at a social function, calling his office at 9:00 P.M. to be sure he's working, looking for lipstick stains, or going through his mail.

### 8. *Take the high road with friends and family.*

You may not get along with every one of his family members or friends. However, be careful not to criticize them in front of your husband. Always take the high road. Realize that he knows them in a special way that you may never understand. How would you like it if he found fault with your chatty but good friends or your meddling sister? Find an impartial friend to air your grudges with. Even if you're absolutely right, try not to complain to your husband. He shouldn't think of you as a grievance collector. Collecting grievances isn't healthy, so be careful not to fall into this bad habit.

### 9. *Try to compromise.*

You want to live in the city. He likes the suburbs. Your idea of a good meal is in a fancy French restaurant. He likes burgers and fries. You enjoy mushy movies, he likes horror movies with blood and gore. What to do?

Be open to new experiences. Broaden your horizons and see what you can learn from him. Maybe you'll learn to like scary movies. Failing that, remember why you married him and that being together is more important than anything in particular you do.

As hard as it may be, let him win sometimes. Why? Because your relationship is more important than always winning. Being a good sport will make you more desirable to him and he is more likely to feel that any man would be lucky to have you. He'll be more afraid of losing you because you're so wonderful to be around. He'll feel that you're easygoing, a summer breeze, not a tornado. It's a good spiritual exercise to compromise and the happiness it brings means you always end up winning in the end.

10. *Be quick to say you're sorry, preferably first.*

Fighting is a normal part of married life, but *Rules* women try not to yell all the time, nurse grudges, hang on to resentments, or turn a minor argument into a major ordeal. When you have a fight, try not to be mean or spiteful. Don't go to bed angry and try to make up first. You'll be glad you did.

11. *Be neat.*

This rule may sound trivial in the light of deep relationship issues, but practical ones do matter to men, even more than to women. Clutter, old newspapers piled around the house, stains on the carpet, runs in your stockings, dirty bathtub . . . all of this is not sexy! You'll feel better when you're organized, neat and clean, and he'll respect you more because you respect yourself. After all, what can he think of you when you don't love yourself enough to wear pantyhose without runs or hang up your clothes?

Married women who are not naturally neat should consult those who are. Get tips on cleaning out closets and filing papers, or hire a cleaning lady. Cleanliness is sexy!

12. *Be independent.*

Don't talk constantly about your fear of being alone or that you could never make it on your own. Your husband should know that you feel you are desirable, a creature unlike any other, "a catch." Men really want women who can live without them, but have *chosen* not to. Don't flip out (in front of him) if you hear about a couple getting divorced. Don't say, "Oh my God. That's horrible. I just don't know what I'd do, I'd die without you!" Calmly say, "I feel so bad for them. I hope things work out," and then change the subject.

13. *Have time out together.*

If you have children, make it a point to hire a baby-sitter and go out for dinner with your husband on a regular basis—without feeling guilty! Of course your children deserve your attention, but they also need to grow up with parents who have a healthy established relationship. Strive to create a sound balance, bearing in mind that time apart from them is as important as time with them.

14. *Lock the bedroom door.*

Your children may initially feel left out and throw tantrums. But when they grow up, they'll remember that their parents had special times together. They'll be better equipped to create intimate marriages themselves.

## 15. *Say things nicely.*

Nothing dampens a loving relationship like yelling or finding fault. If you are annoyed, overwhelmed, or stressed, try to vent your feelings by taking a jog, talking to friends, or doing yoga so that you don't take it out on your husband. Even if you are frazzled, try not to pick on your husband or point out his weaknesses. For example, if you come home and he's put the baby's diaper on backward, don't make him feel bad. Say something positive like, "Wow! It's interesting how the diaper works no matter which way it's put on." Thank him for helping and gently show him the right way. He'll appreciate your gratitude—and he'll get it right the next time!

## 16. *Don't have exaggerated expectations.*

If he's working overtime on weekends or didn't get you *exactly* what you wanted for your birthday, don't get all bent out of shape. Ask yourself, "How important is it?" When little problems bother you, try to be grateful that you are happily married!

# Chapter 21 ——————————

# *Rules* for the Bedroom (When You're Married)

If you want to have a happy marriage, remember to make time for your sex life! You played hard to get, you got him, now make the effort to maintain a healthy sex life with him.

Make your sex life a priority, even if you had a long day at work or your kids were unusually demanding and sex is the last thing on your mind. Or, you may be having one of those superugly, bad hair days. You don't think you look very sexy and sure don't *feel* sexy. Okay, every woman has days like that. We say, try to make the time and be loving anyway!

In addition, be realistic about sex. You may want your time together to be just right—unhurried and romantic. That's not always possible—so try to be flexible. Sometimes sex is the culmination of a beautiful, enchanted evening. At other times, you just seize an opportunity— i.e., in the morning before the kids get up.

You may have a lot on your mind. You're thinking about your sales presentation due the next morning, your kids, how the house needs straightening, and so on. *Let it go.* We all have thoughts whirling in our brains. You don't always have to have an uncluttered mind to have sex. Sometimes sex can unclutter it!

Some women use sex as a bargaining tool. This is a bad idea. If you are trying to make a point, use a different method to get your message across. Don't make his favorite pasta or go with him to the football game. It's not healthy for your relationship to use sex as a weapon, as a way to hurt him. Remember, he can go to the football game with one of his friends, but when it comes to sex, you're the only one!

Of course, if you *do* have the time and the energy, may we suggest you make sex extra special by creating a romantic evening? Take the silver candlestick holders you received as a wedding present out of the closet and cook his favorite dinner, play some soft music, wear his favorite outfit, and be loving. Once in a while, you could ask your parents or in-laws to watch the kids and plan a romantic weekend getaway.

You'll be happier—in the long run—if you have a healthy sex life! Here are seven reasons why:

1. It will help keep your commitment to each other strong!
2. He'll think about you more often during the day.
3. He'll appreciate your thoughtfulness.
4. He'll be less likely to stay late at the office.

5. He'll always want to be with you or call you.
6. He won't be so grouchy. (Big smile.)
7. You won't be so grouchy. (Even bigger smile.)

Always be pleased and flattered because your husband *wants* to have sex with you. In a *Rules* marriage, your husband comes to *you* for sex and you're both happy.

# Starting Over—*Rules* for the Mature Woman

If you are an older woman, *The Rules* may come as no surprise to you. You probably agree with our ideas more than your twenty-five- or thirty-five-year-old daughters. After all, when you were dating thirty or forty years ago—before the full advent of feminism, dutch treat, and the sexual revolution—*The Rules* was the accepted way to date. It was the *only* way. Back then, you didn't call men, ask them out, sleep with them on the first date, or live together before marriage. You didn't think twice about it either, it just wasn't done!

But that doesn't mean you did *The Rules* in their entirety, and it doesn't mean you don't have things to learn, especially if your first marriage was a disaster.

Your mother may have told you not to chase men, but did she tell you to pursue a career and/or interests, to develop boundaries and self-esteem, and not to make a man the center of your life or accept his bad behavior? Did she tell you to marry for love (not just to get out of the house or to be taken care of financially)? If she didn't, you need *The Rules.*

We have heard from older women who said that their first marriages ended in divorce—not necessarily because they pursued their husbands, but for other reasons that simply would not have occurred if they had done *The Rules.*

For example, they married a good friend—someone whom they felt affection for, but not passion—and their marriage and sex life reflected it. They married for financial security and were miserable emotionally. They married because of social pressures to do so—they didn't want to be spinsters. They did not recognize the signs, or they chose to ignore them. They thought, "My love will change him," and married an alcoholic, a gambler, or a womanizer and lived to regret it. Love was not enough. They didn't create an interesting life of their own and became completely dependent on their husbands, which drove them away.

These women did not necessarily chase these men, but they did not do *The Rules* either. *The Rules* are not just about getting married, but about marrying Mr. Right and having a fulfilling life of your own.

So if you find yourself in the dating market again because you are divorced or a widow, use what your mother taught you—don't chase men—but also do *The Rules*—create a life of your own and only date and marry men you truly care for who treat you well. Don't marry believing you will change him. If he is a little abusive or puts you down in any way before marriage, it will only get worse.

If you are from the old school, not calling a man or sleeping with him on the first date is probably easy for you. So you must work on other changes that could prevent you from catching Mr. Right.

For example, have you stopped caring about your appearance—gained weight, stopped wearing makeup, cut down on salon visits?

If you're divorced, are you bitter about men because of your failed marriage? Or too eager and available (not challenging and mysterious) when men do show interest?

If you're a widow, do you feel hopeless about finding a love as great as your first husband? Have you stopped socializing? Or when you do go out occasionally, are you unenthusiastic?

If some or all of the above is the case, here are some rules for you to work on:

*Don't let yourself go.* Remember, you are a creature unlike any other. This rule applies to older women as much as twenty-five-year-olds. It has nothing to do with age. It's mental. Think you're beautiful and worthwhile . . . and you will be! Think positive. Keep your mind occupied with interesting ideas, activities, people, and reading material and you will be interesting. You'll have something to talk about on dates other than your doctors' visits and grandchildren.

Whatever you do, don't neglect your appearance. There is no reason you shouldn't do everything you can to look attractive. Don't console yourself with excess food or alcohol or painkillers. Eat right, exercise daily, and wear pretty clothes. Read books by Helen Gurley Brown *(The Late Show)* and Joan Rivers *(Bouncing Back)* that focus on being positive and exercising to fight off aging. Try to emulate them or anyone else you know who is your age and in good shape. Be old-fashioned about dating, but youthful about your attitude and looks.

*Socialize.* You must. If you are recently divorced or widowed, your feelings probably range from lonely and lost to bitter and confused, especially if your husband died or left you for a younger woman. You might be suffering from grief, fear, and panic. Perhaps you haven't dated in thirty years and don't know where to begin. Of course, you must allow yourself time to grieve—grieving is natural and healthy—but don't let it go on too long.

If you want to remarry or at least have a loving companion, you must make every effort to meet men. Instead of believing that your life is over and all you have to look forward to is grandchildren, tell yourself that there are plenty of divorced men and widowers out there, and go where you can meet them.

We understand that this is not always easy or pleasant. You would much rather stay at home and watch TV, call your children, knit, cook, or read a book, but don't become a recluse, or spend every free evening going to the movies and dinner with other women. Don't bury yourself in canasta, card games, or mah-jongg with your single friends. These are all pleasant ways to pass time and you should do them sometimes, but they are no way to meet men!

Motivate yourself to take social actions by thinking of spending your old age with a loving man, not only as a companion to your married couple friends and your children. Think of how a romance will brighten up your life, and the benefits of spending nights, weekends, and vacations with a man.

Where to meet men? Try everything. Go to museums, church/synagogue, vacations/cruises for your age group, or get involved in a charity or a sport such as golf where men are sure to be found. You must force yourself!

Be on the lookout for men who are newly single. Keep in mind that men who have been married for most of their adult lives are often lost and searching for someone to fill that void. Show up wherever they may be found, but remember, they must approach you!

If you can't find a woman to go to social events with, go alone. In fact, you might be better off alone! Older men who are themselves not so confident socially may feel uncomfortable invading a group of women. So if you do attend a party or lecture with a group, at least stand a little apart from the other women you came with so you look approachable. Take care to appear relaxed no matter how you really feel. For example, don't clutch your pocketbook tightly against your chest as if you are trying to ward off a mugger.

*Be happy and carefree on dates.* You probably have had your share of life's difficulties and maybe even some physical ailments. Possibly you're worried because your daughter is getting divorced, your back bothers you, your husband died and left you with big bills, you have high blood pressure, or had a brush with cancer. You may have plenty to complain about, but try to complain to your women friends, not to a man you are dating. Be cheerful and light. Don't let him think that you are desperate to remarry, concerned about money, or feel lost without a man. It's not good to seem desperate.

Once you start dating someone you like, almost all *The Rules* apply:

Don't call him—of course, you already knew that!—but you *can* return his calls. While older men enjoy the chase, it's a different kind of hunt. It's no longer a bungee jump! They're not looking for that kind of a thrill. They're not trying to have children with you. They're older, they're tired, they've been through many things, so you can call them back . . . the next day. (Try to use the twenty-four-hour rule; wait twenty-four hours before returning the call.)

Don't accept a last-minute date and don't see him unless it's for the weekend. If he's always asking you out for tea on Tuesday, he doesn't think you're that special or he has a girlfriend. Let him pick you up and take you to dinner.

Don't mention your children or grandchildren and show pictures of them or ask him to meet them unless he suggests it, and don't ask about his children or ex-wife

133

unless he brings them up. Don't volunteer information about your ex-husband. If he asks about your divorce, just say the relationship didn't work out. If you are a widow, don't get too emotional or show how much you are suffering. This will be hard, but you must!

Keep it casual in the beginning and end the date first. Wait until you are in a committed relationship—he is calling you regularly and asking you out for Saturday nights for several months—to become very involved or go away with him.

Don't buy him expensive gifts or pamper him, even if you are a wealthy woman and can afford to do so. Also, if you have more money than he does and he wants to marry you, don't be shy about asking him to sign a prenuptial agreement. (Of course, if he asks you to sign a prenup, go ahead. You are not marrying for money.)

Older women might not necessarily want to remarry. The reasons are usually children and money. But if you do want to get married and he doesn't, then you must pull back a little—stop seeing him for a few weeks, go on a separate vacation, give him an ultimatum, whatever shakes him up a little—and see how he responds.

If getting remarried is not that important to you—if it's love and companionship you want, not a wedding and lifestyle that you crave—then it's fine to live with him or go steady forever! You can act married—go away on vacations together and split the expenses. You can even spend a whole winter with him in your condo in Florida.

So long as he is calling you, making you feel special—

weekend dinners and flowers on holidays—and is civil to your children, you don't have to walk down the aisle again. For you, the second time around is about having someone you love who loves you to spend your golden years with.

## *Chapter 23* _____

# *Rules* for Same-Sex Relationships

Do *The Rules* apply to same-sex relationships? If so, how? Do both people do *The Rules*? Or one? Which one?

Confused? Don't be. It's really quite simple. It's a self-diagnosable problem. If you are reading this book or this chapter right now, you probably can apply *The Rules* to your life!

If you read *The Rules* and identified with the feelings of hurt and abandonment that come when a relationship ends and thought to yourself, "I wish they would put in a same-sex chapter because if they substituted a few words I could really relate!", then you do need *The Rules*!

Everyone who is gay or lesbian knows whether or not they are the kind of person who needs structure, some sort of self-protection, in a relationship. If you are this type of person, you're probably very sensitive. You think a lot—obsessively may be more accurate—about the other person and the relationship. You get down—really down—when overlooked or rejected. You're not the type who *naturally* moves on. You don't think breakups are for the best. You think they are downright devastating!

Perhaps you've been hurt before, or experienced a lifetime of hurts, not to mention the social pressures that go along with being gay. You *want* to be in a loving relationship, but you can't bear getting hurt again. Then *The Rules* are for you.

Much of the focus on gay issues has been on coming to recognize and accept one's individual sexual identity, not on how to *behave* in same-sex relationships. This chapter attempts to fill that void with some sound advice.

*The Rules* can work like a charm when used by individuals who want to know the "how to" of dating when they are completely at ease with their sexuality but at an emotional roadblock as to how to proceed. Do you ask someone out or wait to be asked? Should you play hard to get?

Don't think there aren't any rules. There are, it's just that there's a little more camaraderie and mutuality in same-sex relationships than in male-female relationships. You can show some interest, you can return some phone calls. It's not so one-sided. There's more balance.

When you go out to places alone or with friends, you're open to meeting someone, you're just not desperate. You don't aggressively approach anyone at a party. You smile back if someone smiles at you, and if someone moves a little closer to you, you give a "It's okay to move in closer" smile. You want to let the person know you're approachable, that you are open to the idea of meeting someone. But that's all.

Eventually a conversation begins. It's going well. You're both animated. You laugh, at the room, at the night, at the jokes, but you don't bare your soul, your feelings. You're lighthearted. You come on slow, not like gangbusters. You're not *too much, too soon.*

Being gay or lesbian, perhaps you've felt a little isolated or separate your whole life. You've been waiting to meet someone who "understands." But when you do actually meet someone special, don't reveal too much—find a good friend or therapist to share your intimate problems with. Don't unload all of your past history on a new person for they will probably be overwhelmed by your intensity. Worse, they may be very happy to have you depend so much on them, but it will create the kind of codependent, needy relationship you *don't* want.

It is very hard to keep from sharing too much when you find someone who is receptive. After all, there aren't a lot of people who understand what you have had to go through. But motivate yourself to use restraint with the knowledge that you are building a solid relationship and sparing yourself the pain that accompanies the inevitable end of an overly dependent one.

So, be casual. The person must give you signs that they would like to get together again. You will get a *feeling.* It's different from a male-female relationship because if the man doesn't ask the woman out, that's it, it's over. In same-sex relationships, the lines are a little more blurry, but rules still exist, and following them is not as hard as you think.

Pace the relationship. Get to know the person you're interested in slowly—don't spill all the beans during a three-hour coffee date. You are drawn to the person, but you don't bare all. Wait as long as you can, knowing that the more mysterious you are, the better.

The idea is to bring the *spirit* of *The Rules* into your dating life. You should *never* pursue anyone relentlessly. If there's no mutual interest, no give and take, then there's nothing. If the person you're involved with seems to enjoy being the pursuer, that's great and actually makes things easier. You enjoy being pursued and you're sure of their feelings for you so you're less anxious.

Regardless, don't stay on the phone for hours and don't see the person at a moment's notice. You have a life, you have other plans, you are not waiting to be rescued.

Don't feel pressured to have sex right away. Don't see this person all the time or live together until you're exclusive.

Maintain your self-esteem and self-respect. If the other person has a wandering eye, neglects you, or constantly makes sexual comments about other people when you're around, move on to new possibilities.

You know that a relationship without boundaries, without give and take, is not a relationship that is worth having. Perhaps you've settled before. Now, armed with *The Rules,* you don't want anything less than lasting, secure love. You want the best. You *deserve* the best, and by following *The Rules,* you will get the best!

# *Rules* for Personal Ads and Dating Services

If you are planning to use personal ads, voice-mail ads, video dating, or matchmaking services to meet men, we recommend that *you* place the ad and let men respond to *you*.

Why? It goes back to the basic premise of *The Rules*: man pursues woman. He must search through a sea of print ads, voice mails, or video images and pick *yours* out. He has to like *your* hair color, *your* distinctive voice, the way you wrote *your* ad, *your* height and profession, and so on. Remember, he's the hunter! Every man has a type, a voice, or a look he likes. There has to be a spark for him that attracts him to you, something that makes him find you unexplainably special.

We have found that responding to a man's ad doesn't seem to work as well. Answering his ad, liking his type, liking his voice or looks, or what he does for a living puts you in the unwanted position of being the pursuer. In addition, he'll know you are interested in him or his type and the challenge will be over.

Of course, even if he picks you out and likes you, there's no guarantee that you'll like him. But this would also be true at a bar or a party. You wouldn't go up to the guy who's "your type"; but you would wait for a man to approach you. The same pretty much applies to dating services and ads, although it's not quite as black and white.

You just need to keep going on dates until a man who responds to your ad is someone who appeals to you. Hopefully, you are getting lots of responses from men—see tips below for placing an ad that draws the most letters—and have many choices. Having many men to choose from is always good—the more dates you have, the more practice you will get, and you will be less inclined to get hung up on any particular man.

What should your ad say?

To get the most and best responses, your ad should be short, light, flirtatious, and focused on your physical attributes, not your feelings.

Any man responding to your ad wants to know, first and foremost, what you look like. If you are placing a print or voice-mail ad, you must give him a mental picture of you.

You may find it difficult to describe your appearance. If so, one method we've found to be effective is to say which model or actress or well-known personality you resemble. Don't lie, but don't be modest either. Hasn't anyone ever told you you look like someone famous? If you're tall, blond, and slim, try to think of a well-known model with those attributes. If you are short with dark hair and big eyes, perhaps there's a movie star or TV sitcom character you resemble. Ask your friends to help you come up with someone who you could honestly say you look like. Put it in your ad. Men love this stuff!

Limit your ad to about four lines and stick to the facts—age, height, profession, hobbies. Don't say you're looking for true love or romance. He should think you're just dating.

Here's a good voice-mail ad:

"I'm twenty-eight years old, five feet seven inches with long brown straight hair and green eyes. People tell me I look like (model/movie star). I'm a dental hygienist. I like tennis and swimming. Well, that's me! [Giggle] Have a great day."

Here's an ad you would *not* want to use, even if this is exactly how you feel:

"At the end of my rope. It's really hard to meet men so I decided to try this. I'm thirty-five, a financial analyst, looking for someone to spend the rest of my life with. I'm not into playing games."

Aside from the fact that a man seeing or hearing this has no idea what she looks like, the ad is much too serious, too revealing, and quite depressing.

When you receive responses, call the men you are interested in meeting when you think they will not be home and leave your name and phone number on their answering machine. Of course, if he answers, only stay on the phone for ten minutes.

Assuming you get his machine and he calls you back, still don't stay on the phone for more than ten minutes. Hopefully he will set up a date to meet you within that period of time. If not, hang up after ten minutes anyway. Staying on the phone longer to give him more time to ask you out is not *The Rules.* Don't become best friends on the phone. We know women who stayed on the phone for hours getting to know men who answered their ads. These men never even asked to meet them, or they made tentative plans and then didn't follow through. They proved to be complicated or unreliable. In cases where a relationship did start, it usually fizzled within a few months. There was no mystery, no buildup—it was simply too much too soon. This won't happen if you're getting off the phone in ten minutes. Get to know him on dates.

So if you don't have many blind dates and you haven't connected recently with any men at singles events, work, or the gym, you should most definitely try personal ads and dating services. The men who respond to ads and sign up with services are usually serious about meeting someone and often marriage-minded—otherwise, why would they spend the time or money? In fact, we know several women who met and married men through ads and dating services.

In conclusion, our advice is to try *everything* until you meet Mr. Right! Remember, placing an ad or joining a dating service does not mean you should stop going to parties, bars, resorts, singles weekends, or take up a social sport like tennis. The bottom line is: *Never give up and never stop trying!*

# Chapter 25 _____

# *Rules* for On-line Dating

Dating on the Internet has become so popular in recent years and we have received so many requests for *"The Rules* way" to go about it, that we felt the subject deserved its own chapter.

So what do we think of on-line dating? To be perfectly honest, while we encourage you to try it if you haven't been able to meet men any other way, we have found that these relationships usually don't pan out. At best, women end up with male friends or pen pals, not husbands.

The main problem with on-line dating is that the relationships are based on chatting—not physical attraction, the spark so necessary for a *Rules* relationship.

In addition, on-line dating can be downright *dangerous.* You have probably read articles about women raped or killed by men they met through the Internet. The truth is, no matter how nice, interesting or sincere the person seems to be on-line, all you know about him is

144

what he tells you. He could be a lunatic, a rapist, a killer, a teenager having fun, or a married man—you just don't know!

Of course, we understand why some women prefer dating on the Internet to the singles scene. They are fed up with finding Mr. Right at bars and parties. If they don't feel attractive, they think they are at a disadvantage in social situations. They believe that they have a better chance of attracting a man with their mind, great personality, or witty way of writing, than their looks. The Internet allows them to date with no makeup on and in sweatpants.

We understand how they feel, but we just don't think this method works as well as face-to-face meetings. The best romantic relationships start out with physical chemistry. Internet relationships are based on chatting. We know several women who spent months talking to men on the Internet before meeting them. Few of these relationships worked out. He calls you his "soul mate," the one who knows his innermost thoughts and dreams, and then marries someone else he's really attracted to!

But if you are determined to meet men on-line, we suggest that you do *The Rules* the best you can so you don't waste time conversing with men who will never marry you or putting yourself in danger. Here are some suggestions:

1. Once he's shown interest in you—responded to your personal ad or approached you in a chat room—tell him you'd like to exchange photos by E-mail right

away. There's no point in continuing an on-line romance if he's not attracted to you.

2. Once he's seen your photo, it's up to him to suggest meeting you. (If he doesn't, then he's not crazy about your looks and it's next!) If he lives in another city, he should visit your city. You don't visit him. (See Chapters 6 & 7: *Rules* for long-distance relationships.) We've heard about women who "hop on a plane" to meet a man they've been chatting with for weeks or months. *Rules* girls let men visit them! When he hops on a plane or drives to visit you, you must meet at a public place. *He should not know where you live!*

We cannot stress the safety factor enough. We've heard about women who risked their lives because they invited men they met on-line to their apartment on the first or second date. This is dangerous. In addition, make sure to give a friend or relative any information about the date—who, what, where, when—so he or she can keep track of your whereabouts.

3. Don't use the Internet to have heart-to-heart conversations or to bond with a man. Many women think that *The Rules*—i.e., don't open up too fast, be honest but mysterious—don't apply to on-line dating. They wonder how they can get to know this stranger if they don't tell him their whole life story right away. They think nothing of baring their souls or discussing their past relationships and their desire to meet and marry Mr. Right. And if he lives in another

city and they don't see him that often, they feel that justifies frequent E-mails.

Don't kid yourself. E-mails are no different from phone calls, letters, and greeting cards. We don't call men, we don't write them letters or cards, and we don't overdo E-mail.

Whether you are dating on-line or face-to-face, men are still men. They do not fall in love with and marry the women who send them the most revealing and most frequent E-mails, even if they say that's what they want. They might tell you that they like women who are honest and open, who say they want a commitment if they want a commitment, who don't play games. But they actually *chase and/or marry* women they are physically attracted to who are elusive and challenging and whose E-mails are as well. Short and sweet is always the best.

If you're on the computer chatting with him so much, how challenging are you? How interesting can your life be if you are glued to your terminal and have time to chat with him ten times a day?

Let him get into the habit of E-mailing you interesting tidbits about his day without necessarily receiving a response every time. Remember, on-line or in person, you are a creature unlike any other and worth pursuing, so let him.

# Chapter 26 _____

# Use a *Rules* Support Group

Let's face it, doing *The Rules* is not easy! Holding back from calling a man you like, resisting the urge to sleep with him on the first or second date, keeping from telling him everything about yourself right away, and all the other rules require tremendous self-control, patience, and faith in this process. The *Rules* may feel like a very strict diet or giving up smoking. If you are used to doing things your way, we encourage you not to do *The Rules* alone!

We strongly suggest you form or join a local *Rules* support group—much like a weight-loss group or Smokenders—that meets regularly to reinforce *The Rules*, or at the very least, get phone numbers you can call. It's easy to rationalize breaking rules—calling a man who hasn't called you or living with a man who won't marry you—when you're doing it alone. But having *Rules-*

minded women to call or a group to discuss your dates with and report to every week makes *The Rules* harder to break. It helps you be true to yourself and *The Rules*.

Besides, you will experience tremendous comfort, hope, and relief when you meet and share your experiences with other women who have gone through what you have gone through with men and are now committed to dating a better way. Being part of a group or simply calling like-minded women will be especially important if your friends, coworkers, or family members don't understand *The Rules*. Talking to other women who do understand will make you feel better and not so alone. Helping other women not break rules—i.e., literally staying on the phone for ten minutes explaining to someone why they can't call him until the urge to passes—will make you stronger and reinforce your own commitment. It's putting money in the bank for a big withdrawal one day!

It has been gratifying for us to watch *Rules* groups form in cities around the country, to hear about women (perfect strangers!) calling each other and networking to do *The Rules*—their only bond being their desire to stop dating in a manner that doesn't get results. They are united in their common goal: to be in loving relationships and marry Mr. Right. Of course, the group fosters close female friendships as well. Some of these women have become good friends who go on singles trips together to meet men, and eventually attend each other's weddings. Being part of a *Rules* support group is an experience you don't want to miss!

How do you start a support group?

If you have friends, acquaintances, or coworkers who believe in *The Rules,* invite them to your apartment for a meeting. If you do not know any *Rules* followers, you can write to us (see back of book) and we will be happy to provide you with the names and phone numbers of *Rules* girls in your area.

Other ways to find women for a *Rules* support group:

1. Make up a flier. For example, one leader of a *Rules* support group photocopied the following message and posted it on kiosks, bookstore bulletin boards, and other prominent spots around her neighborhood:

   "Many women today grew up in the '60s and later, where 'free love' and nonexistent boundaries were the fad. '*The Rules*' show women how to set up good boundaries and build a full life for themselves. Living a joyous and fulfilling life makes women radiant, very attractive, and feel great. So if you want to be a *Rules* woman, contact_____."

2. Try to get free publicity by sending fliers to your local newspaper to run an item in its singles/personal ads section or local radio station. You may find a female deejay at a radio station who thinks your group is interesting, worth promoting, and be helpful to you!

3. Post fliers at health clubs, bookstores, churches/synagogues, and wherever else single women might see them.

4. Contact singles organizations and dating services and ask them to tell their clients.
5. Ask your therapist to start a group.
6. If you are in high school or college and want to start a group, ask your guidance counselor/psychology teacher if you could use a classroom where the group can meet. Explain that there are rules for high school and college students and how students could benefit from a *Rules* group.

Once a group has been formed, we suggest that you try to meet at the same time every week or every month. It's up to you where you meet. If you know one another, meet in someone's apartment. If you're strangers, you're better off meeting in a public place, such as a coffee shop. Some groups meet for lunch or dinner and then go to the movies. Saturday afternoon for an hour or two is a popular meeting time since most people have the day off and it's a great way to prepare for a Saturday night date. Other groups meet on Sunday afternoon and analyze the previous night's dates.

You'll find the group works best if you pick someone to be in charge—to call on people and field their questions. Bring copies of *The Rules* and *The Rules II* to the meeting in case you need to refer to them to answer questions. If the group cannot figure out the answer to a question, suggest the person call or write to us. Some groups have actually booked a group consultation by phone with us during their meeting, with each woman asking a question or two.

The format of the group is entirely up to you. But keep in mind that *Rules* support groups should not be group therapy sessions for discussing one's childhood, money, career, or body image issues, unless these issues are blocks to doing *The Rules.* Some groups are in fact led by therapists or social workers, but the meeting should still focus on *The Rules,* your dating history, and how you are doing them today. It is the leader's job to make sure attendees stick to *The Rules.*

One way to get the group going is to have everyone take turns sharing which rules they did and didn't do that week.

You can raise questions, such as:

What rules are you having a hard time with?

Is anyone thinking of asking a man out?

Or, you can ask hypothetical questions, such as:

If a man leaves his umbrella in your apartment after the third date, what should you do? (*The Rules* answer: Don't use it as an excuse to call him. Wait until he calls *you* and then mention it.)

Encourage women to keep a diary of how they are doing *The Rules.* You could use *The Rules Dating Journal* that asks you to write about your dating history and to keep track of how you are doing *The Rules* day by day (i.e., Who talked to whom first when you met? Has he ever said "I love you"?).

Group members should exchange phone numbers so you are able to call one another in between meetings. These phone numbers will come in handy when you feel compelled to call a man! If a woman is married or living with a man, it might be better to call her at work. Be sure to ask if it's okay to call her at home. You don't want her husband or boyfriend to get upset when he hears messages about playing hard to get!

*Rules* support groups are intended to be free of charge so that those who can't afford private consultations can get help. However, sometimes an organizer will charge participants a nominal fee to cover costs such as postage, phone calls, meeting rooms, and coffee.

Even if it's nothing organized or planned—no fliers, no leader, no format—just a person whose *Rules* knowledge you trust or you and five of your favorite gal pals meeting on Sunday for brunch and talking about *The Rules,* it's still a *Rules* support group . . . and it can really help, so use it!

*Chapter 27*

# *Rules* for Girlfriends, Bosses/Coworkers, and Children

Because *The Rules* work so well with men, many women have asked us if there is a way to apply *The Rules* to platonic relationships with other people, such as girlfriends, bosses, coworkers, and even children. Absolutely. *The Rules* can be applied to other people so that you have good, healthy relationships, are well-liked, and not taken for granted. Here are our rules for other people:

*Girlfriends*

1. Do *The Rules* with men. By doing *The Rules* with men, you automatically become a good girlfriend. Think about it. You're not canceling plans at the last minute to accept a date with a man. You take your plans with your girlfriends seriously—you don't break them for a better offer. You're loyal. Of course,

you're not sleeping with, chasing, or flirting with your girlfriend's boyfriend or husband. You're trustworthy.

2. Figure out who your friends are. You don't want to become a doormat. For example, if you're the one giving all the time, calling, lending your clothes, books, money, and makeup, and getting little or nothing in return, pull back a little and see what happens. It's not good for you or her if the relationship is one-sided. Maybe she's not that interested in the friendship. On the other hand, if *you* are the one always taking, try to give more or not accept as much.

3. Don't be a burden. If you're going through a particularly hellish time—man, health, work issues—don't dump it all on one friend, day and night. Try to complain to several friends so that no one takes the brunt of it and you don't lose friends. Try to give back an hour for every hour they give of their time. Always remember to ask how they're doing, even if you *know* they're doing better than you. Everyone gets their fair share of good and bad in life. It all evens out in the end. To compare is to despair!

4. Be happy for your friends. If your girlfriend is getting married and you don't even have a boyfriend or she lands a great job and you hate yours, it may be hard to feel genuinely pleased by her good fortune,

but you must work on summoning up these feelings. Maybe she was lucky. On the other hand, maybe she worked hard for her success—took more social actions and sent more résumés than you did. It doesn't matter. Whatever the reason, she is your friend and she deserves to feel that you are happy for her, not jealous. Rather than seethe with envy, see what you can do about meeting a man and finding a better job of your own. Send her a congratulations card and smile at her wedding. Wishing others happiness is the best way to ensure our own.

*Bosses and Coworkers*

1. Don't act too casual or talk about your private life at the office. You might think talking about personal matters or your feelings at work will make you feel more at home. But your boss and coworkers will respect and trust you more if they sense that you are professional and not the gossipy type.

2. Work for the good of the company, not for your own personal gain. Everyday think, "How can I contribute to my company or help customers?" Don't think we're being corny or naive here. We know that business can be cut-throat. But when you think of the company, you automatically succeed.

3. Don't focus solely on how to get a raise or a promotion or how to do the least amount of work without getting found out. Think about doing quality work

and being a good worker, or you won't feel good about yourself.

4. Don't be over-eager or volunteer to do too much too quickly in an effort to make your boss notice you. He'll find you if he needs you; be available when he does!

5. Don't be a self-centered, short-term thinker. Everyone around you will smell self-interest and think less of you.

6. Be a team player.

7. Don't work round the clock. Have a social life. Remember that work isn't everything; you will be a much better worker if you are happy in other areas of your life.

## Children

Children are a lot like men. They'll take advantage of you if you let them! One of the benefits of having a *Rules* marriage is that your kids tend to treat you as nicely as your husband does. They copy his behavior, making him their role model for how to treat you.

For example, if your son observes his father being loving and attentive and buying you cards and flowers, he will try to do the same in his own way (i.e., break his piggy bank for a bracelet or bouquet of flowers).

In *The Rules,* we said, "when he loves you, he loves your kids." We would like to add, "when he loves and respects you, your kids learn to love and respect you."

In addition, here are some rules to make sure your children treat you well:

1. Don't let your children treat you as their equal. For example, if they call you by your first name, don't answer. Instead ask, "Did someone say something? I respond to the name Mom." That way they know you're the boss.

   Similarly, don't *ask* them if they want to go to school, brush their teeth or go to bed. Tell them what they must do. Children respond well to discipline and orderliness. You are doing them a disservice when you let them run the show.

2. Don't spoil your kids. You might be tempted to overdo, particularly if you waited until later in life to have children or had to adopt or overcome infertility problems. You might want to jump every time the baby cries. Assuming the baby is fed, dry, and not sick, you do not have to spend endless hours pampering him or her, or you will become trapped in a pattern that's almost impossible to break. Encourage your child to be self-sufficient. As your children get older, encourage them to help with household chores. If you let your children have some responsibility, instead of constantly doing everything for them, you will help to foster independence and competence.

3. Don't make an issue out of food. Don't force them to finish every meal; you may unknowingly begin a lifetime of weight problems for them. Unlike adults, children eat when they're hungry and stop when they're full. They won't starve to death. Save your energy for more important matters like teaching them good manners and values.

4. Have a life! Don't feel guilty for working, talking on the phone about business or with friends. You are entitled to some time to yourself, and you'll be a better mother for having a full life. Mothers who spend too much time with or overindulge their children and neglect themselves are often frustrated and resentful. It's not necessarily the quantity of time you spend with your child, but the quality.

   In the same vein, let your child know it's not okay to interrupt you when you have company or are on the phone. Unless it's an emergency or your child is hurt or sick, tell him or her that you are busy and will talk to him or her later—and make sure you stick to your word. This way your child learns to respect your private life and learns patience. He or she will get mommy time, just later.

5. Don't buy out the toy store. You might be able to afford the best of everything, but should you buy it? We think not, unless you want your child to turn into a monster, the kind of kid who throws tantrums in a department store. So even if you can afford the

whole store, restrain yourself. The same goes for pushing your child to participate in every hobby and sport. Check your motives. Are these really your child's interests or your ego at work?

6. Let your children take responsibility for their actions. If your children don't want to do their homework, try to find out why; perhaps they didn't understand the assignment. Help them, but don't do it for them. If it's just a case of being lazy or willful, tell them they are responsible and they will have to face the consequences. If you want you can explain that you did your homework when you were growing up and that's how you got to where you are today.

7. Stick to your word. Explain to your child if he/she engages in bad behavior—i.e., curses, hits someone, or acts out—he/she has to suffer the consequences. You decide what the punishment is—i.e., no TV—and stick to it. If you make idle threats, you will lose credibility and your children will get away with murder.

8. Encourage your child to confide in you. Lay down the law about good and bad behavior, but *always* leave the door open for your child to tell you something you may not approve of. In other words, be strict, but not judgmental. That way if there's something your child doesn't want to tell you, he/she can at least tell you that much, i.e., "I have a secret I

don't want to tell you." If you don't want to find out about your child's problems too late or from someone else, make sure your child knows that he or she can always confide in you and count on you *no matter what.*

A general tip: Good mothers are observant mothers. If you sense that your child is anxious or edgy, perhaps you want to cancel your social plans or leave work early to spend "a kid day" or "kid's night out," something as simple as pizza and a movie may get him or her to open up and tell you what's going on.

# Don't Worry, Even Men Like *The Rules*

In case you forgot, you're doing *The Rules* because it's good for *you* and your self-esteem. Whether men like or dislike *The Rules* is irrelevant. The truth is, men can talk about wanting to date in an open, up-front, rational way, but what they *respond* to is altogether different—they respond to challenge, mystery, and intrigue. If a man likes a woman, he'll call her again. If he likes her and she doesn't let the first date become a marathon, he'll want to see her again that much sooner. He'll lose interest if she breaks rules, regardless of *what he says!*

But you are probably curious what men think and say about *The Rules* anyway. We have found that, if presented correctly, most men don't find *The Rules* objectionable at all. They actually like the results *The Rules* produce.

Here is what men have told us in their own words:

"If I met a woman and thought she was The One, I wouldn't let any book she was studying get in the way {of pursuing her]," says an executive at a university in New York.

He believes that men feel "cheated" of the chase and "refuse to commit" or demand "space" when women break rules.

He is not alone. We have received dozens of letters and calls from men thanking us for writing *The Rules* and letting us know that they are buying copies for their daughters, sisters, female friends, and ex-girlfriends.

A teacher from Lexington, Kentucky, wrote to say that he loved our description of a *Rules* girl—"busy, with high self-esteem, not sleeping around or chasing married men, having values and ethics, and loving with her head and her heart. That is a very attractive woman to any sane man . . ."

An M.D. from Chicago, Illinois, wrote to say that he was "always getting into relationships with codependent women who had no lives of their own. These women were unusually clingy and bordering on being fatal attractions. Now, I have a renewed sense of hope in finding a woman who possesses the qualities of a *Rules* girl."

Yet another male *Rules* fan from Los Angeles wrote, "You are right—it is more exciting for us men when the girl is hard to get. I have never been interested in any girl who chased me. Flattered yes, but not interested."

An Illinois medical student who is planning a career in psychiatry wrote, "In my opinion, any young woman who knows and uses *The Rules* correctly will have a tremendous advantage in finding and keeping successful long-term relationships."

Of course, there are men who think *The Rules* are just silly—not offensive, just silly! These men simply cannot believe that women read such books. But they don't realize the extent to which women can obsess about relationships. If a man actually *knew* how much a woman thought about him, a relationship gone wrong, or lost herself over a breakup with a man, he would really encourage her to do *The Rules.* He'd say, "Well, go ahead then, read that book if it helps!"

So even if your boyfriend suspects you're doing *The Rules,* even if you think he'd be mad if he found out about it—so that's why you don't call me!—still do *The Rules.* Don't talk about it. Deep down, a man would rather you do *The Rules* than not, *no matter what he says.* Deep down, every man would rather marry a girl who gives him space and lets him breathe. So don't worry about what men think about *The Rules,* just do them. Men *do* like *Rules* girls—in fact, they do more than like them—they love and marry them!

# *Rules* Tips for Men

We wrote *The Rules* to help women enjoy dating, not to confuse men. But since *The Rules* was published, quite a few men have contacted us. Some have called, some have written us letters, and some have even attended *Rules* seminars.

Why? Well, some men simply wanted to thank us for telling women what they knew to be true about relationships. Others expressed confusion about *The Rules* and what "dating in the nineties" should be like.

Some men wanted to know how they should behave in relationships and exactly how to tell if a woman they were dating was interested in them. This was not really news to us. We had heard that men were actually asking women who wouldn't call them or wouldn't go out with them, "Are you doing *The Rules* on me?"

Some men suggested that we write a book or a chapter called "*Rules* for Men." They wanted answers, insights, clues, anything really—most of all, they wanted to be included! This was not entirely news to us either. We had heard about and witnessed men poring over *The Rules* in bookstores or borrowing the book from female friends to pick up pointers, to understand women—and themselves—a little better. We had also heard that some men were blaming *The Rules* when a woman refused to go out with them.

Therefore, we have written this chapter to address men's concerns, to include them, to dispel any tensions between the sexes, and to explain why they should not blame *The Rules* for a woman's lack of interest. We never meant to create any conflict between men and women. We don't think relationships should be adversarial. We want men and women to make happy couples.

Hopefully you will find the following useful!

### How To Tell If She Is Interested

She's interested in you if:
1. She gives you her phone number *if you ask for it.*
2. She declines to take your phone number or business card, but is willing to give you hers *if you ask for it.*
3. She says "yes" to a Saturday night date if you ask by Wednesday.
4. She says "I'd love to, but I can't," if you call too late in the week or she is truly busy.
5. She seems to have fun on the date, laughs, lets you kiss her good night. Maybe you're not sure if she'll

marry you one day, but you definitely get the sense that she'll probably see you again.

6. She doesn't call you back all the time, but when you get her in, she's happy to hear from you.

7. She doesn't stay on the phone for too long—but when she gets off she is always nice about it.

She's *not* interested in you if:

1. She says "no" when you ask for her number or offer her yours.

2. She says "no" when you ask her to dance at a party.

3. She says "no" or "I don't think so" when you ask her out *early* in the week for Saturday night—several weeks in a row.

4. She *never* returns your calls, *ever!*

5. She says "I don't feel a spark" or "I'm not interested" or "please don't call me again."

# Chapter 30 _____

# *The Rules* Are a Healthy
# Way of Life

At first glance, you might think that *The Rules* are just a practical guide to dating—no more, no less. But if you take the time to think about it, you'll see that *The Rules* help you with more than dating—they assist you in establishing a healthy, balanced lifestyle.

By not pursuing men or allowing yourself to rationalize staying in a dependent or destructive relationship, you automatically become a healthier, more grounded and self-empowered person. You're not a nervous wreck, trying to get a man who isn't interested in you to love you or begging the man you are dating to make a commitment.

If you have ever chased after a man you were in love with but who did not share your feelings and who eventually rejected you, you will know what we're talking about. If you're like most women, you took a long time to recover. The relationship took its toll on your work, your sleep, your appetite, your friends, and your nervous system.

A *Rules* girl does not initiate or stay in a bad relationship out of fear of being alone and low self-esteem. She has enough self-confidence to trust that the right man will appear in her life, and she knows if she walks away from a relationship that is going nowhere, something better will take its place. Being optimistic, growing, changing, striving for the best are all wonderful by-products of *The Rules.* Believing in the abundance of the universe— that there are plenty of other fish in the sea!—is a sane and healthy attitude to take.

Of course, even in good relationships, women can become quite obsessive, wanting to call their boyfriends or husbands all the time or act overly dependent and needy. By sticking to *The Rules,* these women learn not to call so often and are encouraged to pursue independent interests, form friendships, and become more self-sufficient so that they don't end up believing that they are "nothing without a man." Depending too much on any person is not good for you.

By doing *The Rules,* you learn the value of leaving men alone sometimes. Everyone benefits. The man is grateful to be left alone to watch the ballgame or whatever else interests him, and you have more time to read a book or cultivate your own interests. *The Rules* trains women to practice self-control, to concentrate on matters other than "the relationship." Perhaps by not seeing him all the time or getting too wrapped up in his life, you will find your energy going into something useful. Maybe you will find yourself calling a girlfriend or a charity that really needs your help—and that's a much more productive use of your time than fixating on whether or not to call a handsome stranger or the man you are involved with.

When you do *The Rules, you live and let live*—and you yourself will reap the benefits of your forgiving behavior. *The Rules* also encourage you to cultivate healthy coping skills. Take this example: You've had a fight with your boyfriend. You think it's life and death. You want to resolve it immediately by spending hours analyzing your relationship with him. He doesn't want to. He'd rather shoot hoops with the guys to get the anger out of his system and then discuss it with you quietly over dinner and a movie.

Let him play ball. Let him handle the fight in a way that is comfortable for him. Don't try to make it happen your way all the time. If you need to talk about it, call a good friend or your mother. He'll work through it in his way; you'll talk it out in yours. Little fights stay little this way, and don't escalate into big ones.

Sometimes the best way to resolve disputes is *not* to talk about them, especially if *he* really doesn't want to. Many women love to talk about the relationship, but big discussions can give most men a headache. Trying to get him to talk every time won't necessarily bring him closer, but might drive him away. Demanding that he read relationship books or attend relationship workshops may be what *you* like and good for *you,* but it might be boring for him, so *focus on yourself.*

Sometimes the best way to mend a fight is to do something thoughtful. Be loving, wear a nice outfit, give him a backrub, have a romantic evening together. Paradoxically, you might learn that when you don't nag him to talk about the fight when *you* want to, he is more likely to bring it up or say something loving when *he's* ready.

When you do have a disagreement, as we say in Chapter 20: "A *Rules* Refresher for Married Women," if at all possible, try to be the first to say you're sorry. You'll feel better in the long run if you apologize, take the high road, and forgive and forget. Your boyfriend or husband will appreciate your willingness to patch things up. Don't stand on ceremony, waiting for him to do it. Why ruin your serenity with resentment and sleepless nights? Don't think we are being naive here. We know that men are not always right and that it's sometimes hard to forgive and forget. But try—you'll be amazed at how much better you feel when you don't hold on to your anger!

We have also shared our philosophy with women who, because they did not know about *The Rules,* have had bad experiences with men—men who stopped calling suddenly after a long-term relationship, cheated on them, or treated them disrespectfully. Understandably, these women feel bitter, which is certainly not a serene way to live.

Of course, we acknowledge their pain—there is nothing more devastating than being hurt by a man we love. But we try to discourage these women from acting on their feelings. We tell them that *The Rules* are never about hurting others or getting even—i.e., sending men hate mail or harassing them with phone calls. Instead, we focus on ourselves, we evaluate our part in the breakup, we see where we broke rules, and how we tolerated bad behavior. *We change.* That's why we encourage women to get their anger out in therapy or a *Rules* support group.

It is important to realize that you can't *make* a man treat you well or marry you, you just have to do *The Rules.* We help these women see that by not doing *The Rules* in these relationships, they helped place themselves in a position to be hurt. For example, one woman simply ignored the fact that her boyfriend of fifteen months only asked her out every *other* Saturday night and had never told her he loved her or mentioned marriage or the future. She thought he had "trouble expressing his feelings." She was devastated when she found out that he was actually seeing other women. If she had known about *The Rules,* she would have seen the warning signs.

We tell these women that the best action they can take is to do *The Rules* on the next man they meet! Living well is the best revenge! To let go of the past and move on are empowering! Or as we say in *The Rules, Next!*

However, even though we know *The Rules* work, we don't force them on our friends or anyone else for that matter. *The Rules* is all about leaving men and other people alone. We're tolerant, not judgmental. If someone is having trouble with men, we're happy to share our method, but that's it. We don't preach.

Perhaps you know of a woman—a friend or a coworker—who is suffering in a relationship because she is not doing *The Rules.* You keep telling her to do *The Rules* but she thinks it's silly or just not for her. You bought her the book, you invited her to a *Rules* support group, you've even said

"I told you so" when her boyfriend forgot her birthday. What should you do?

The next time your friend complains that her boyfriend of three years still hasn't proposed, be sympathetic, as if she had called you to say she's in pain from spraining her ankle while in-line skating. Say, "Gee, that's too bad." Don't say, "Well, if you just did *The Rules* . . ."

She is more likely to do *The Rules* if you don't preach. She is more likely to do *The Rules* if she sees them work in your life. So leave her alone and invite her to your wedding. By just doing *The Rules,* chances are you will become a healthy influence in her life.

# Answers to Frequently Asked Questions About *The Rules*

**Q: If I do *The Rules,* how will he know the real me?**

A: On dates you *are* yourself. There's a big difference between being mysterious and being deceptive. You don't lie, you just don't open up too fast. You don't say you went to an Ivy League school if you went to a community college. But you don't bring up subjects that would tip your hand, such as marriage, the future, children, or feel you have to answer questions that would reveal too much too soon or make you uncomfortable.

For example, if he asks why "a nice girl like you is not married," you can casually say, "I really haven't thought about it" and then change the subject. Don't say anything depressing like, "I haven't been on a date in six years" or "It's really hard to meet men." Don't say anything cynical like, "I guess I'm just lucky."

The point is, you don't have to answer every question

he asks you. Your dating history is none of his business on the first, second, or third dates. Realize that if he really presses the issue, he probably is either not that nice, or not that interested in you. When a man is interested in you, he doesn't want to make you uncomfortable.

Don't worry, "the real you" will definitely shine through. Your conversation, your appearance, your laugh—all of these are uniquely yours, and will help him to discover the creature unlike any other that is you.

**Q: If I do *The Rules*, how will he know I like him?**

**A:** You say "yes" when he asks you out by Wednesday for Saturday night. You show up on the date—you smile, you're warm and pleasant, fun to be with, you thank him for a nice evening. That's how he knows you like him.

Contrary to popular belief, you do not have to call men or send them thank-you notes or buy them presents for them to see that you are interested.

If you like him, but he calls too late in the week for you to accept the date, you say, "I'd love to, but I have plans." By saying "I'd love to," and declining nicely, with genuine regret, he'll know you would actually like to spend time with him, you're just busy. If he likes you, he'll call again. But next time it will be earlier in the week.

**Q: What do I do when a man gives me his business card and says "Call me?"**

**A:** Look at the card as if no man has ever given you one before, smile, and sweetly say, "No thanks. I don't think so."

*Rules* girls don't call men and have no use for their business cards or phone numbers. If a man is really interested in you, he will then ask for your number. Don't say, "I don't call men. It's better if you call me." That's telling him what to do. He either asks for your number on his own or he doesn't. You only want men who *want* your number.

**Q: What if a man leaves a message on your answering machine on Wednesday? Can you call him back to secure a weekend date?**

**A:** In the first month of dating, it's best not to call him back at all. This way he'll have to call again (at the beginning of the following week) if he really wants to see you. Better to lose one Saturday night date than show too much interest and risk destroying a potentially long-term relationship.

The first month should establish a pattern: he is the hunter—calling you and calling you, if only to just find you in! Better that he keep trying to pin you down and not actually reach you in time for a Saturday night date than your calling him back right away and being readily available. By not calling back, some women we know didn't actually have dates with men for a month or so, but now they're married to them. They set the chase in motion and created longing.

Of course, if he calls you two to three times in one week and still gets your machine, a quick call back can be okay. Use your common sense. Remember, we said you should *rarely* return his calls, not *never!*

After the first month, you can return his calls a day or two later or call him occasionally (say, once for every four of his calls), preferably when he's not home. If he absolutely insists that you call him, call once in a while so that he doesn't think you're not interested.

**Q: If a friend sets you up on a blind date and the date goes very well, do you call the friend to thank her and to tell her you like him?**

**A:** No, don't call the friend to thank her or express interest in the person she introduced you to. This may sound harsh or rude, but *The Rules* answer is to make a mental note to do something nice for the friend in the future. To call and tell is to kiss and tell. She'll either inadvertently mention to him that you called or possibly call him to tell him so, and he'll definitely interpret it as a sign of interest. Let *him* call her to find out what you thought of him. If your friend does ask, you should keep your answer as evasive as possible. For example, you can say, "He seemed nice! We had fun." This is noncommittal but positive—just the tone you want to take.

## Q: Do *The Rules* work on *all* men?

**A:** Fortunately, yes. *The Rules* work on all men from all countries and from all walks of life. And that's actually a good thing. It means we don't have to rewrite *The Rules* for every nationality, or every time we meet a man or figure out how the man we're dating is the exception to *The Rules.*

We do not have to initiate relationships with ˙shy men" and only play hard to get with corporate titans. We believe all men like a challenge and that men are not shy when they see a woman they are attracted to. If they don't make the first move, it's because there may be no spark and they are simply not that interested! The same man you think is shy will jump on a plane to be with the woman he's crazy about. The same man you've chased for five years and called "commitment-phobic" will marry another girl in six months.

Women try to tell us otherwise. We've been told some men are withdrawn and that's why women have to approach them. We've been told some men are talkative, so how can one get off the phone in ten minutes? We've been told some men need women to mother them because they didn't get enough attention or nurturing as children. Yet these men do not necessarily marry their "nurturing" girlfriends, but the women who were slightly aloof, laughed, and didn't play savior, the girls who didn't care too much too soon.

That's why you should do *The Rules even* if you meet a man in a relationship workshop or a program where feelings are freely discussed and defenses are down. A man is still a man and still likes a challenge *even* if he attends weekend seminars on self-improvement or goes to Tibet for spiritual healing. That means that even if he "opens up too fast" and talks about his feelings right away, you should still be "honest but mysterious." *The Rules* supercede any philosophy, therapy, or religion he may be involved in because he's a man before he's anything else!

So rather than trying to figure out every man's ethnicity, character, or upbringing, simply do *The Rules* on every man you meet. You will have plenty of time down the road to be his salt of the earth, his Rock of Gibralter, and his soul mate when you're married!

**Q: My problem is not *The Rules,* but finding men to do them on. Any suggestions?**

**A:** *The Rules* is not a guide to finding eligible men, but how to behave once you've met them. But since so many women have asked for help in meeting men, we'd like to offer some suggestions.

Two thoughts to get you going: Your chances of meeting a man greatly improve when you leave your apartment, so get off the couch! And remember, you only have to find one!

Also keep in mind that you shouldn't go out blindly, but try to go to places that singles frequent, not married couples and/or kids.

So why don't you try?

1. Club Med or any singles vacation.
2. Church or synagogue or other place of worship.
3. Jogging in the park.
4. Joining a gym.
5. Taking up a male-dominated sport such as golf, scuba diving, tennis, or skiing.
6. Putting a personal ad in a newspaper or magazine.
7. Signing up with a dating service.
8. Joining a ski house.
9. Meeting friends for dinner at a trendy restaurant (where men hang out at the bar), instead of a diner.
10. Going to a lecture or book signing that would draw men.
11. Taking a summer share.
12. Asking friends to fix you up (but don't be too aggressive about it).

However, wherever you go, whatever you do, don't talk to any man first, *sit or stand next to him* hoping he'll notice you.

**Q: If I can't talk about my feelings or my past relationships on dates, what can I talk about?**

**A:** Sports, politics, your favorite books and movies, museums, the Internet, work, weather, and dining (the restaurant, the meal, the ambiance). Dating is not a therapy session—talk about subjects outside yourself. There's a whole world out there!

Q: The book is so popular, what if a man asks you point blank, "Are you doing *The Rules* on me? Is that why you don't call me?"

A: You could say, "What rules?" and hope he thinks you've never heard of the book and drops the subject. Also remember, just because a man asks a question doesn't mean you have to answer it. But if you feel compelled to say something, you can say, "Actually, I'm just not a big caller." Before reading *The Rules,* you called men more often, now you don't. We've all read advice books that have deeply influenced us and incorporated some of their ideas into our lives until it *became* who we are. Now it's *part of your personality* to rarely call men! (Besides, no one can *prove* you're doing *The Rules*!)

Q: How do I know if he's The One?

A: If you are feeling ambivalent, we suggest you ask yourself these questions: "Do I like to kiss him? Can I wake up with him for the rest of my life? Do I like his voice, talking to him, the way he dances, the way he treats people? Do I like the way he treats me? Do I like him as a person?" The answers to these questions really matter on a day-to-day basis. *You have to really like just being with him!*

Of course, we cannot tell you how to feel about a man, but it's best if you feel something like, "Wow, I've got to marry this man! I must be with him." If you are tortured, confused, or have to make a list of his pros and cons, it's not a good sign. If you're forcing yourself to like him because he *appears* to be the proper match (your mother loves him, your friends say he's perfect for you, and he makes a good living) but he's not your type, you may be settling. Trust your gut feelings!

Q: I went out with a man who at the end of the date said he had a great time and would call again. He never called. Why? It's been a month. I thought I did *The Rules*. May I call him to find out what went wrong?

A: Don't be surprised. We hear from many women who have this happen to them. Some men are just being polite when they say it. Some had a good time, but didn't *really* want to go out with you again. A *Rules* girl doesn't spend a whole lot of time trying to figure it out. She moves on . . .

We don't recommend calling him for an explanation. It's simply not *The Rules* to chase a man or put him on the spot. And what could he possibly say without hurting your feelings? But if you absolutely must call, wait a considerable amount of time until you're sure he's not going to call you, then go ahead. Better to break *The Rules* with this (dead) man than with a real candidate.

Q: How can I meet his parents and friends before he meets mine if he moved from L.A. to New York and everyone he knows is on the West Coast?

A: Hold off for as long as possible from introducing him to your family and friends before you meet his. If he's truly in love, he'll probably tell his parents about you and they may book a trip to New York to meet you. Or, since he's living in New York he has probably established his own "New York family"—close friends, his boss, coworkers—so at least wait until after he introduces you to them.

Q: You have a date for Saturday night, but it's Saturday afternoon and he still hasn't called to confirm. Do you call him and ask, "What's up? Do we still have plans?"

A: No, you *act as if you knew* you had a date, and be dressed and ready to go when he does call or shows up at your door. In other words, he should never know that you wondered all day (and possibly all week!) if you'd ever hear from him again. If he doesn't call and forgot the date, don't call him. Just know that one day he could forget your wedding date. *Next!*

Q: At a party, is it okay to make eye contact or smile at a man?

A: You can look at him if he looks at you. By all means, smile back if he smiles at you. You just don't initiate anything, from flirting to standing in front of him to make him notice you. On the other hand, you don't have to look down to avoid his gaze if he stares at you, or turn your back to him. You're polite, you just don't pursue men!

**Q;** I don't like to give out my home number to a man I just met. Is it okay to take his number and call him?

**A:** While we understand the safety reasons for not giving a stranger your home number, we're not fond of this approach. It throws off *The Rules.* How do you know he was really going to call you? Sometimes a man doesn't know how to say, "It was nice meeting you. Have a nice life." Instead, out of politeness, he says, "Can I have your number? Maybe we can get together sometime." You say, "Well, actually, I don't give out my number. Why don't you give me yours?" You call him and feel justified in doing so. After all, he did *ask* for your number. And then you wonder why the relationship doesn't work out.

We suggest you try to figure out a way for men to get in touch with you first—whether it's by giving them your work number or getting a personal voice-mail number— so that they can make the first move. That way you keep your privacy, but you can still do *The Rules.* Of course, if there is no other way, try to wait a week before you call him. But keep in mind, even if you call him, he must still be the one to ask you out. If he hasn't done so within ten minutes, end the conversation and move on. If you *do* go on a date, and after spending several hours with him you still feel uncomfortable giving him your number, you probably have reservations about him and might want to move on to someone you do feel comfortable giving your number to.

# Chapter 32

# A Final Bonus— 20 Extra Hints

1. You just found out about *The Rules* but you're already in a relationship. What can you do? Start doing *The Rules* today! Yes, you can do *The Rules* midstream. Starting right now, don't call him, don't beep him, and don't stay on the phone for more than ten minutes when he calls you. If you are seeing him every night, see him only once or twice a week. If he asks why, you're busy, busy, busy! If he asked you to go away for a week, tell him you can only go away for a three-day weekend—your job is hectic, that kind of thing. If you're living with him but you don't have an engagement ring or a wedding date, start looking in the real-estate section of the newspaper for an apartment. Get the idea? Whatever you're doing, cut back. If you're giving too much or losing yourself, pull away and see what happens!

2. On dates or in phone conversations, don't use the words "nurturing," "relationship," "bonding," or talk about getting your needs met. You don't want to sound like a walking relationship book. In the early stages of dating, staying light is essential.

3. Make sure whatever message you record on your answering machine is sensible and in good taste, not outlandish. In the course of returning hundreds of women's phone calls, we have heard pretty crazy stuff—everything from wild cowboy music to the lyrics of very sensual songs to special holiday greetings. Outrageous messages show that you are trying too hard and that can easily alarm or turn off some men. You don't have to express your creativity on your answering machine. Err on the conservative side. A pleasant message is usually the best, something like: "Hi. You've reached Karen. I can't come to the phone right now. Please leave a message."

4. Don't be jealous if your boyfriend or husband's ex-girlfriend calls him or sends him letters. As long as *he's* not initiating the calls and letters, you have nothing to worry about. No one can take away what's yours!

5. If you're on the phone and he calls on the other line, do not get off the phone every time for him. You don't want to seem too interested or the kind of woman that will cut short an important call with a

friend or business associate the second a man calls. Just tell him, "Oh, I'm on the other line. Can you call me back in ten minutes [or whatever time is convenient for you]?" That way *you* don't have to call him and he calls *you* again, but make sure to be available when he calls back.

6. Don't send a man letters, brochures, or newspaper/ magazine clippings that you think they'd be interested in. Tell a friend or *Rules* support group member that you were going to send them these items and then throw them away. Men can find this kind of attention too intense. Sometimes they don't even acknowledge it or bother to thank you. You might think they're rude or didn't receive the material. The real reason is you overwhelmed them!

7. If you think a man is doing *The Rules* on you because he's pulling back, ending the calls and dates first— he probably isn't. He may just not be that crazy about you. When a man loves you, he just wants to be with you. If he doesn't seem to be pursuing you, he probably isn't really interested.

8. If you are doing *The Rules,* but aren't getting any dates, the problem may not be *The Rules.* (In other words, don't use this as an excuse to ask men out.) You must either go out more often—try personal ads and dating services—or consider improving your appearance, if necessary. Try wearing contact lenses in-

stead of glasses, try working out more often or eating less if you're not in great shape, or updating your wardrobe. Keep working on yourself, look your best, and the men will come!

9. Now that *The Rules* is a best-seller, a man might have heard of it and think you are doing *The Rules* on him. Not to worry. Even if he does suspect you're doing *The Rules,* it won't reverse its effectiveness.

10. How to compete with all the *Rules* girls out there? You don't, except to keep doing *The Rules.* When a man likes you, he likes *you.*

11. Remember to say "please" and "thank you" on dates as well as to friends, family members, and business associates. *Rules* girls are a refreshing breed—they're polite! They value themselves and the people they come in contact with.

12. The first or second date can be a Thursday or any week night. But the third date *should* be a Saturday night.

13. Remember, if he's attracted to you and you're quiet on the date, he thinks you're not a big talker. If you're not his type, he thinks you're boring. This just goes to show you, you don't have to try too hard.

14. If he's dating others, you should date others as well. We're not exclusive until *he* wants to be exclusive and *he* brings it up.

15. Try not to speak to him every day. If you're following *The Rules,* you're seeing him once or twice a week for the first month or two. But what if he's *calling* every day, or several times a day, just to chat? What if he beeps you every day? Should you speak to him every time? No, you shouldn't be that accessible. Leave your answering machine on at home sometimes and say it's hard to talk at work. You don't have to return his beeps—let him get into the habit of beeping you to let you know he's thinking about you without necessarily getting a response. You should be busy and mysterious. If you've been talking daily, talk every other day (when he calls). The rest of the time, he should get your machine. Let him miss you. If he wants to talk to you several times a day, let him marry you!

16. Don't tell men you're doing *The Rules.* Do not explain or discuss *The Rules* with men, and don't tell them how to date. We've heard stories of women who actually tell men, "You have to call me by Wednesday if you want to see me Saturday." That's not *The Rules.* That's revealing your hand; it's like wearing a slip without a dress. *The Rules* answer is to tell a man who calls late in the week, "Thanks, but I have plans."

He must figure out that if he wants to see you on Saturday, he'll have to call you earlier in the week. We can't make a man really interested in us by telling him when to call. He either is or isn't. You'll find out fast by doing *The Rules*.

17. Don't go away with a man for a week. Save it for your honeymoon! What if, after dating Mr. Right for a month or two, he invites you on a cruise or to an exotic island for a week? *The Rules* answer? You're busy and can't get away.

    Cruises and weeklong vacations make men go backward! Things can get hot and heavy when you see each other seven days a week, twenty-four hours a day. You might act too wifey—telling him to watch his fat intake or giving him advice about a family or business problem. He might be romantic on the trip, but pull back when you return, saying he needs his "space." You may not hear from him for a week or two. The only big trip you should take is your honeymoon. He can take you for an overnight or weekend trip occasionally after dating you for three or four months, but that's it!

18. How to end a relationship or stop seeing someone who you like but aren't crazy about? As soon as you're sure he's not for you, just say, "I think you're great, but I just don't feel a spark" or "I don't think this is working out for me." It's not good for you to tie yourself up with someone you don't love—and it's

not good for him either. If he really cares about you, you could end up leading him on and preventing him from meeting someone else. That's not fair. Remember, following *The Rules* saves you both a lot of heartache.

19. Don't have more than one drink on dates so that you do *The Rules*, end the dates first, and, most important, remember what happened!

20. Remember, Cinderella ended the date first!

*Chapter 33* _____

# Success Stories: Women Who Followed *The Rules* and Changed Their Lives!

*S*ince The Rules *came out in February 1995, thousands of women have contacted us to ask for help with this successful dating method and to share their experiences. Around the world, women are buying* The Rules *for themselves as well as for their single friends and forming support groups to help one another follow* The Rules. *Mothers are sending* The Rules *to their daughters and grandmothers are sending it to their granddaughters. The word has gotten out.* The Rules *work! Here are some true success stories that may inspire you to do* The Rules *better—or for the first time!*

*Jennifer T.'s story, Los Angeles, California*
    *When she stopped sending a doctor greeting cards and gave him space, he decided she was The One.*

Jennifer T., thirty-three, called us from Los Angeles to ask for our advice. A friend sent her *The Rules* and she was anxiously trying to practice them on Mark, a thirty-one-year-old doctor, divorced for two years. She said that after four months of dating Mark, he started pulling away. She wanted to know what she was doing wrong. She was crying when she called us—she really wanted to marry this man!

We went over all the important facts—how they met, who pursued whom, what rules were broken—to pinpoint the problem.

They met on a blind date. It was instant attraction. Mark called her *early in the week* for Saturday nights for the first two months. A good sign. They started seeing each other once or twice a week. They had sex after three months. So far, so good. But one evening over dinner, Mark told her he wasn't sure how he felt and what the future would bring. What went wrong?

After some close investigation, we discovered Jennifer had strayed in several key areas. Her major slip was actually after the second date. She sent him a romantic card saying that she was glad they met and signed off with, "XO, Jennifer." Mark didn't acknowledge the card. After spending a weekend in Aspen a month later, she sent him a second card thanking him for the trip. Again, he never called to thank her for the card.

Of course, *Rules* girls know not to send men thank-you cards. They simply thank a man in person after the date or the weekend. Putting it in writing is not necessary, shows too much interest and effort and possibly low self-esteem. He got to spend time with you! Who needs a thank-you card for that?

A romantic thank-you card tells a man exactly how you feel and destroys the mystery and challenge of pursuing you. *Rules* girls *receive* cards, they don't send them. Mark never sent her a card, much less said, "I love you."

Jennifer's other mistakes: After seeing Mark for two months, she started to accept last-minute dates on Monday nights. And when Mark told her he wasn't sure how he felt, she asked him a lot of questions to get him to pinpoint the problem. What wasn't he sure about? Was there something he didn't like that she could change? Did he still have feelings for his ex-wife?

Mark said it wasn't anything in particular. He suggested they "take a break" for a week or two so he could sort out his feelings. Jennifer was devastated.

This is what we told her:

When a man says he's "not sure how he feels" and wants to "take a break" after dating you for four months, what that usually means is he feels overwhelmed by your interest and intensity. It also means that, because he knows exactly how you feel, he doesn't find you intriguing or challenging. He feels slightly bored or too comfortable, not excited about you. He may even be annoyed that you made the pursuit too easy.

We advised Jennifer not to call or write Mark—she was thinking about sending him an "I'm here for you when you're ready" card. We suggested that she go away with a friend on a singles vacation and take other actions to meet men, so she was busy and not waiting by the phone for Mark to call, or too eager when he did call.

We told her that if and when Mark called that she

sound light and breezy and not bring up their last serious talk, but to turn him down for a date if he asked by nicely saying, "Gosh, I'd love to, but the next couple of weeks are no good." We suggested she end the call in ten minutes, and simply say she was on her way out, if necessary.

The reason is, the only way Jennifer would ever know if Mark loved her and couldn't live without her was to let him miss her. Mark had to feel that she was slipping away and only a declaration of love could win her back. Jennifer agreed, since being with a man who was "not sure how he felt" after four months was just too painful.

Since following this plan of action—dating others, booking a trip to Club Med, turning Mark down for a couple of dates—Jennifer called recently to report that Mark was aggressively pursuing her. For the first time, he sent her flowers and a romantic card that said, "Miss you terribly! Love, Mark." He asked her in advance for Saturday nights as he did when they first met. On the first date since their breakup, Mark apologized by saying, "You know I wasn't sure how I felt before. I guess I needed some time to think. Now I know, you're the one!"

Rather than ask him to elaborate or turn that remark into a serious talk, Jennifer simply smiled. She sent him only one card since they reconciled—a simple birthday card, nothing scenic or too sweet. Three months later, Mark proposed. Jennifer is sold on *The Rules* and telling all her single friends to try them.

*Barbara N.'s story, Athens, Ohio*
  *When she stopped being "friends" with men, she got a friend for life, a husband!*

After reading *The Rules*, Barbara, a twenty-nine-year-old social worker, called us to seek advice. She confessed that her big downfall is becoming close friends with men on the rebound or men who want to talk about their girlfriends and get her advice, and then falling in love with them and getting hurt. Barbara was always caught up in some three-way relationship—waiting for a man to be dumped by the girl he really liked, or playing second fiddle to another girl. In other words, she was constantly accepting crumbs (Thursday night dates and Monday lunches). It was always the same story: These men thought Barbara was nice and sweet, but they never thought about marrying her.

When we told Barbara to stop being friends with men and to quit playing therapist to their relationship woes, she argued that she valued male friendships because she liked to know how men think to help her date better. We told her that all the dating help she needed was contained in *The Rules* and that her future husband would be her best friend. But until then, men should not be her bosom buddies.

We put Barbara on a plan of not getting into any deep conversations with men about relationships—theirs, hers, or anyone else's. We knew this would be difficult. Being a social worker, Barbara loves to talk about this kind of stuff.

We also told her not to call men and rarely return their calls, and not to be so serious. This has been very hard for Barbara who feels it's "rude" not to return calls and "superficial" not to talk about one's feelings. But she agreed to take our advice because her way hasn't worked. She hadn't been in a satisfying relationship in five years and was tired of being alone.

Six months ago, Barbara started doing *The Rules* on Barry, whom she met at a singles bar. He approached her. After about fifteen minutes of light conversation, she forced herself to mingle (even though she would have liked to talk to him the entire night), which prompted him to ask for her phone number. She did not offer him her business card as she usually did, so he flagged down the bartender for a pen to write it down. She couldn't believe it. *The Rules* were really working!

Like clockwork, Barry called her the following Tuesday for a Saturday night date and they have been dating ever since. For the first time, Barbara is not trying to be best friends with an eligible bachelor. She doesn't accept last-minute dates to hang out in his apartment. She ends dates first. If he talks about his problems, she doesn't play therapist. She listens, she sympathizes, she's sweet, but she ends the conversation first.

Barbara used to think that a man would lose interest in her unless she solved his problems. Now she realizes that she doesn't have to be this or that or do anything really, except *The Rules,* to keep a man interested. Now she sees that a man falls in love with a woman's essence. She also didn't bring Barry into her world too soon by introducing him to family and friends before he introduced her to his.

By following *The Rules,* she let Barry simply fall in love with her—and it's working. Barry recently took Barbara as his date to his best friend's wedding. As the bride and groom walked down the aisle, he whispered, "I want the next wedding we go to to be ours."

*Susan G.'s story, Boca Raton, Florida*
*After years of dating Mr. Wrong,* The Rules *helped this divorcee catch Mr. Nice and eventually Mr. Right.*

Susan, forty, a divorced interior designer, has a history of dating men who are moody, sarcastic, and difficult. Her ex-husband, Brian, constantly found fault with her and her last boyfriend, Steven, withheld affection and complained that she wasn't "there enough for him." Susan's response was to drop her friends and hobbies to make him dinner, type his résumé when he suddenly decided to change careers; she even decorated his apartment for free. The more she tried, the more he criticized. He eventually broke up with her.

Susan went to a therapist who concluded that she's attracted to men who remind her of her critical father. But after thirty sessions, Susan's therapist could not stop her from dating such men nor did she offer her specific instructions on how to attract and keep desirable men. She was just good at helping Susan see her destructive patterns.

At the suggestion of a girlfriend, Susan read *The Rules,*

called us, and decided to give them a try. We advised her that in addition to following *The Rules,* she should be on the alert for men who are moody, critical, or difficult even if she was physically attracted to them. This worked. For the first time in her life, she began to date men who treated her well, complimented her, and pursued her without much effort on her part. For the first time, she wasn't jumping through hoops to please a man, but dating with self-esteem.

Susan finally met a really considerate guy, Alan. But she wasn't sure if she liked Alan because he was nice or because she really liked him. Susan was also not sure she even wanted to get married again, but she did want a *Rules* relationship. We encouraged her to write down her feelings so she could see them in black and white and analyze them more honestly.

Susan soon realized she was not really in love with Alan, but simply forcing herself to love "a good guy" because he was treating her well, thanks to *The Rules*! Susan concluded that she did not find Alan particularly exciting, merely kind and considerate. She was just so happy not to be mistreated that she tried to love him. Sometimes when you do *The Rules,* you don't fall in love, but you certainly don't get treated badly either!

Susan agreed with our assessment. And although it was painful to break up with "a good guy," she did it anyway and started dating again. If you're anything like Susan, it bears repeating that *The Rules* are not about settling— that is, forcing ourselves to love a man simply because he loves us or does all the right things, like calling often and buying us flowers and so on. The purpose of *The Rules* is to get the guy you are truly crazy about to marry you.

We assured Susan that by doing *The Rules* on men she truly liked, she would get the big payoff. She would catch Mr. Right. We were right. Susan has since met Robert, who she thinks is really, really sexy, not *just nice*. She thinks about him a lot and doesn't have to ask anyone if he's Mr. Right. He calls her almost every day and makes her feel special.

Susan credits *The Rules* for changing her life. She feels that following *The Rules* forced her to think more highly of herself, to not accept just any treatment from a man.

Susan joined a *Rules* support group—about a dozen women who meet every week in her neighborhood to discuss their particular dating situations and to support one another. Susan recently announced to the group that, after ten months, Robert proposed. He wanted to live together as soon as they had gotten engaged, but she refused, saying she was an old-fashioned girl, so he moved up the wedding date!

*Stacey G.'s story, Houston, Texas*
*She discovered* The Rules *four years after she got married. Better late than never!*

Stacey, a thirty-three-year-old secretary, found out about *The Rules* a little late—four years after she got married! After reading the book, she craved a real *Rules* marriage. If anyone tells you they got married without doing *The Rules*, keep in mind that *The Rules* are not just about getting married, but having a great marriage and a husband who is attentive and really crazy about you!

Indeed, *The Rules* would have saved Stacey much heartache over the years! She met Neil, a cute stockbroker, at a health club. Both are avid exercisers. He approached her at the bicep machine, offered to show her a couple of moves, and then asked her to go for coffee after the workout.

So here we have a good *Rules* beginning—he thought she was beautiful and made the first move. But dazzled by his good looks, Stacey readily said yes and that was her first mistake. She was too eager, too available. She should have said, "Oh, I would love to, but I can't." Remember, we don't go for coffee on a moment's notice! This is not a game, it's because you value yourself and your time. A man has to wait to spend time with you!

That started a year's worth of last-minute dates because Neil realized he could see Stacey without giving her advance notice. Quite often, Neil would ask Stacey for a Saturday night date on a Friday afternoon. She would cancel plans with her girlfriends, only to run into Neil at the gym that Saturday afternoon and be told, "I'm not in the mood. I think I'll hang out with the guys tonight." She'd be crushed, but he was really cute and she thought this was the best way to "get him." If she wasn't always available, maybe he would think she didn't like him, or worse, ask another girl who was available! She'd cry to herself and her friends, but hoped this would lead to marriage anyway.

This went on for about two years. Neil rarely treated

her well. After a romantic weekend away together—her idea—he said to her rather matter-of-factly, "You know, Stacey, I like you, but I'm not sure I'm ever going to settle down. I like my freedom." One Sunday afternoon she came over and offered to make dinner. He said "great" and then left her in the kitchen while he played basketball with his friends. She cooked and cried while he shot hoops.

Not knowing what to do about this going-nowhere relationship, Stacey finally threatened to quit her well-paying job and share an apartment with her older sister in another city. She didn't know she was doing *The Rules*—she wasn't even aware of the concept. She simply had had enough and her sister suggested she give him an ultimatum: either marry me or good-bye. She took the advice. Afraid of losing her and feeling that she had been such a good sport, Neil proposed.

Four years later, Stacey wished she had some of the payoffs of a *Rules* marriage. For example, when they went to a party, Neil was always leaving her side to talk to strangers. At home, he was sometimes affectionate, but didn't try to initiate intimacy. In general, he treated her like good, old dependable Stacey—the girl who cooked while he played basketball—rather than a creature unlike any other.

We advised Stacey to study **Rule #26** ("Even if You're Engaged or Married, You Still Need *The Rules*") and apply them from this day forward. For example, we told her to wear more flattering clothes (she tends to dress conservatively), to join a gym (she stopped exercising after they got married), to leave *his* side and mingle when they go to parties, not to initiate intimacy or hand-holding, not to call him at work so often, or leave love notes on the refrigerator door. We suggested she act a little more elusive—like the girl who threatened to leave town. After all, it was not the "good girl" Stacey who cooked his dinner that made Neil propose, but the *Rules* part of Stacey that finally won him over.

Already Stacey has noticed a difference since applying *The Rules*. Neil calls her more often from work and is more attentive both at home and in public. He recently surprised her by taking her to a romantic inn for her thirty-fifth birthday. Once hopeless about changing the course of her marriage, Stacey is now a big believer in *The Rules*.

*Amy D.'s story, San Diego, California*
*This chronic Rule-breaker learned the hard way: moving to be closer to a man makes him run the other way!*

Amy, forty-three and divorced, felt she finally hit the jackpot. After seven years of being single since her husband left her and in relationships that didn't wind up at the altar, she met Jack on a business trip. Amy and Jack worked at the same computer company but in different offices—she in San Diego, he in Minneapolis. All employees were invited to corporate headquarters in Chicago to learn a new software system.

Amy noticed Jack right away and sat next to him at the seminar. Big mistake! *Rules* girls don't make things happen. A man either notices us or he doesn't, sits near us or he doesn't. Having more software experience than Jack, she offered to give him a few pointers. That's a common ploy smart women use to get a man to notice them. Unfortunately, it never works! Trying to be a gentleman, Jack took Amy out to dinner to say, "Thank you." One thing led to another, a few drinks, and they ended up sleeping together in his hotel room.

The fast and furious courtship continued after the seminar was over. They E-mailed and called each other constantly. He suggested she move in with him and try to get a job in the Minneapolis office. The company didn't have an opening in Minneapolis, but Amy quit her San Diego job anyway to be with Jack. (How many women have thrown away their careers and apartments for a man? Of course, they always live to regret it. *Rules* girls know better!)

The first month or so of living together was pure bliss—he worked hard and she decorated and cooked while looking for work, unsuccessfully. But by the second month, the fun faded. Jack was annoyed that he was supporting Amy. He stayed at the office later and later and called at the last minute to say he wasn't coming home for dinner. On weekends, he left her alone to play golf.

Amy had no real friends in Minneapolis and became increasingly depressed and lonely. She worked up the courage to ask Jack what was going on. He told her "things weren't working out as he expected" and to move out as soon as possible. (When you don't do *The Rules*, men can be pretty cruel. They just want you gone, yesterday!)

Devastated, Amy called a friend in San Diego who offered her a couch to sleep on and a copy of *The Rules*. Amy read it in one sitting and wept, realizing all the mistakes she had made with Jack (and with many other men, including her ex-husband). She spoke to Jack first and sat next to him; she used her computer smarts as an excuse to strike up a conversation; he wasn't really interested in her, just her expertise; she slept with him on the first date, which wasn't really a date, but simply his way of thanking her for computer help. And worst of all, she quit her job and left her family and friends to move in with him.

After reading *The Rules,* Amy started attending *Rules* support group meetings, practiced not initiating conversations with men or helping them with business. She recently met Bruce at a computer trade show in New York City, where he lived. He approached her. After talking for fifteen minutes, Amy told him she had to get going, so he asked for her number. This was radically new behavior for Amy, who pre-*Rules* typically told a man her whole life story right away. After the show, Bruce called her, made a special trip to San Diego to visit her, and sent her postcards in between visits for the first few months. After dating for eight months, he proposed and said he would move to San Diego.

Amy just can't believe it. This is the first time she didn't have to make things happen with a man, the first time she let a man do all the work . . . and it worked! They're planning a June wedding and she's keeping her apartment and her job. For a savvy businesswoman who first thought *The Rules* were for "other women," Amy is now leading a *Rules* support group and loving it!

Do you have a *Rules* story? We would love to hear how you are using *The Rules* to get engaged or married or date successfully. Please write to us at:

**The Rules**
**FDR Station, P.O. Box 6047**
**New York, N.Y. 10150**

# Also Available

*The Rules: Time-tested Secrets for*
  *Capturing the Heart of Mr. Right*
*The Rules Dating Journal*
*Rules Note Cards*

For more information about the following products
and services:

1. *Rules* newsletter
2. Private consultations with authors
3. *Rules* seminars
4. *Rules* audiotapes
5. *Rules* videotapes
6. *Rules* merchandise
   and more

Write/call/fax us: *The Rules*
FDR Station, P.O. Box 6047
New York, N.Y. 10150
Phone: (212) 973-0751
Fax: (973) 422-0048
Website: www.therulesbook.com

Now that you've read *The Rules*, seminars are available to help you do them. For more information, please fill out this form and mail it to:

*The Rules*,
FDR Station
P.O. Box 6047
New York, NY 10150

NAME:

ADDRESS:

PHONE #:

AGE:

PROFESSION: